Martin Luther's Table Talks

Martin Luther's Table Talks

Abridged Edition

Martin Luther, edited by Henry F. French

Fortress Press
Minneapolis

MARTIN LUTHER'S TABLE TALKS
Abridged Edition

Copyright © 2017 Fortress Press. All rights reserved. Except for brief quotations in critical articles or reviews, no part of this book may be reproduced in any manner without prior written permission from the publisher. Email copyright@1517.media or write to Permissions, Fortress Press, PO Box 1209, Minneapolis, MN 55440-1209.

Cover image: Image provided by the Pitts Theology Library, Candler School of Theology, Emory University.
Cover design: Rob Dewey

ISBN: 978-1-5064-3431-5
eISBN: 978-1-5064-4025-5

The paper used in this publication meets the minimum requirements of American National Standard for Information Sciences — Permanence of Paper for Printed Library Materials, ANSI Z329.48-1984.

Manufactured in the U.S.A.

This book was produced using Pressbooks.com, and PDF rendering was done by PrinceXML.

Contents

	Introduction to the Abridged Edition	1
1.	Table Talks on the Life of Faith	5
2.	Table Talks on the Ministry	29
3.	Table Talks on the Word of God	51
4.	Table Talks on the Sacraments	71
5.	Table Talks on Theology and Theologians	89
6.	Table Talks About Martin Luther	125
7.	Miscellaneous Table Talks	155
	Index	189

Introduction to the Abridged Edition

2017 marks the 500th anniversary of what came to be known as the Protestant Reformation, a movement of immense importance in the reshaping of Western religious, political, economic, and social life. October 31st, 1517, is commonly recognized as the beginning of the Reformation. On that day, Martin Luther—an Augustinian monk and Doctor of biblical theology—posted 95 Theses (points for debate) on the door of Wittenberg Cathedral, arguing against what he considered to be the Church's corrupt and unbiblical practice of selling indulgences.

An indulgence was a "purchased promise" that past, present, and future sins would be forgiven and, therefore, purgatory could be avoided by oneself or by one's loved ones who had died but on whose behalf an indulgence was purchased. As Johann Tetzel, a priest and seller of indulgences was reputed to say in his sales pitch, "As soon as a coin in the coffer rings, a soul from purgatory springs."

Luther's study of the Bible led him to insist that forgiveness of sins and salvation could not be sold by the church and bought by ordinary Christians. Rather, he insisted that forgiveness of sins and salvation were the gift of God's grace received through faith and not by so-called works of righteousness (Eph 2:8).

The theological convictions of Luther and other early reformers that shaped the Reformation are often referred to as The Five Pillars of the Reformation—Word alone, Faith alone, Grace alone, Christ alone, and Glory to God alone. In the "table talks" in this volume, you will find these themes woven over and over again into the mealtime conversations around Luther's table.

An early consequence of the developing Reformation was the closing of many monasteries and convents. The Augustinian monks, including Luther, who had previously lived in the Black Cloister in Wittenberg, abandoned the monastic life. Elector (Prince) John Frederick of Saxony, however, gave the place to Luther along with an annual living stipend. Luther continued to live in the Black Cloister, and from the time of his marriage to Katherine von Bora in 1525 until his death in 1546, it was the home of his family.

The spacious building was almost constantly filled by all sorts of people. In addition to Luther, his wife and the six children who were born to them, several poor students roomed and boarded there in return for clerical and other services, and there was a constant flow of guests from near or far.

About five o'clock in the afternoon supper was served in Luther's household. This meal was often shared by exiled clergymen, escaped nuns, government officials, visitors from abroad, and colleagues of Luther in the university who frequently stopped in. The relaxed atmosphere and the warm hospitality of the home was conducive to spirited conversation. A frequent guest at Luther's table, one John Mathesius, left this description of what it was like around Luther's table.

> Although our doctor often took weighty and profound thoughts to table with him and sometimes maintained the silence of the monastery during the entire meal, so that not a word was spoken, yet at appropriate times he spoke in a very jovial way. We used to call his conversation the condiments of the meal because we preferred it to all spices and dainty food.
>
> When he wished to get us to talk he would throw out a question, "What's new?" The first time we let this remark pass, but if he repeated it—"You prelates, what's new in the land?"—the oldest ones at the table would start talking. . . .
>
> If the conversation was animated, it was nevertheless conducted with decent propriety and courtesy, and others would contribute their share until the doctor started to talk. Often good questions were put to him from the Bible, and he provided expert and concise answers. When at times somebody took exception to what had been said, the doctor was

able to bear this patiently and refute him with a skillful answer. Reputable persons often came to the table from the university and from foreign places, and then very interesting talks and stories were heard.[1]

Not surprisingly, some of the people who listened to these conversations at Luther's table began to take notes. There was nothing strange about this. After all, the same persons were taking notes of Luther's lectures and sermons, and they were interested in recording the opinions he expressed at table too. Not everything that was said was noted but only what interested one recorder or another. The notes were taken for private use as personal remembrances of a revered teacher or as guides for the solution of biblical, theological or personal problems, and were not intended for publication.

Although these notes, collected and collated, were first published as a stand-alone volume in 1566 (some 20 years after Luther's death), early editions of Luther's works did not include the Table Talk. It wasn't until a 24-volume edition of Luther's works, published between 1739 and 1753, that the Table Talk was finally included. The reason for the delay? Many Protestants were embarrassed by some things in the Table Talk—for instance, the earthy language which Luther occasionally employed, the severity of his polemical attacks against both religious and temporal leaders, and the freedom with which he criticized the composition and contents of some books of the Bible.

There is a good deal of autobiographical material in the Table Talk. Luther often spoke about his early home and parents, his education, his decision to become a monk, his experience in the monastery, his rediscovery of the gospel, his attacks on scholasticism and the papacy, his journey to the Diet of Worms where he was ordered to—but refused to—recant his teaching, his marriage to Katherine von Bora, and so on.

You will also find in the Table Talk, brief biblical exposition, snippets of doctrinal teaching, comments on ministry, the church and the sacraments, and pastoral counsel on living as a Christian. There is also much about the political, economic and social world that Luther lived

---

1. Georg Buchwald (ed.), *Mathesius' Predigten über Luthers Leben* (Stuttgart: Paul Rocholls Verlag, 1904), 155–56.

in—a world very much unlike our own. It is good to keep in mind that these are tidbits of conversation over dinner.

The conversations throw light on Luther's temperament and nature and variously reflect his humor and anger, his cheerfulness and melancholy, his candor and liberality, his critical acumen and credulity, his gentleness and blustering defiance.

The present volume is an abridgment of Volume 54 of the American Edition of Luther's works, which is itself an abridgement of the six volumes of Table Talk in the German Edition. In Volume 54, the talks are arranged in 9 chapters, each chapter devoted to talks recorded by one individual. Within each chapter, the talks are arranged chronologically, the result of which is that disparate Table Talks follow each other throughout the book.

This volume arranges the Table Talks thematically within seven chapters. In abridging the 500 some pages of Volume 54 to this slim volume, much had to be left on the cutting room floor. The selections were made with the general reader in mind, not the scholar. The reader whose interest is piqued by this sampler of Luther's table conversations is encouraged to move on to Volume 54 of Luther's collected works.

A final editorial comment. Words enclosed in brackets are always additions inserted by the translator. In some cases, these are variant readings from one or another early manuscript. Most of the words enclosed in brackets were added by the translator to suggest the probable meaning of otherwise obscure texts.

And now, to the table.[2]

Henry F. French

---

2. Portions of this Introduction have been adapted from the Introduction to Volume 54 of the American Edition of Luther's Works (Minneapolis: Augsburg Fortress Publishers, 1967).

1

Table Talks on the Life of Faith

God's Grace Is Hard to Believe

Between November 30 and December 14, 1531

"It's very difficult for a man to believe that God is gracious to him. The human heart can't grasp this. What happened in my case? I was once terrified by the sacrament which Dr. Staupitz carried in a procession in Eisleben on the feast of Corpus Christi.[1] I went along in the procession and wore the dress of a priest. Afterward I made confession to Dr. Staupitz, and he said to me, 'Your thought is not of Christ.' With this word, he comforted me well. This is the way we are. Christ offers himself to us together with the forgiveness of sins, and yet we flee from his face.

"This also happened to me as a boy in my homeland when we sang in order to gather sausages.[2] A townsman jokingly cried out, 'What are you boys up to? May this or that evil overtake you!' At the same

---

1. This incident probably occurred on June 7, 1515. First observed in 1264 as a day to commemorate the institution of the Lord's Supper, Corpus Christi was marked by a solemn procession in which the host (the body of Christ) was carried. Corpus Christi is the Latin for body of Christ.
2. In Luther's youth, when mendicancy was a way of life, it was customary for students to support themselves by begging for food. Like other forms of begging, this practice was forbidden where the Reformation was introduced.

time, he ran toward us with two sausages. With my companion, I took to my feet and ran away from the man who was offering his gift. This is precisely what happens to us in our relation to God. He gave us Christ with all his gifts, and yet we flee from him and regard him as our judge."

The Character of Neighborly Love

April, 1532

"One ought to love one's neighbor with a love as chaste as that of a bridegroom for his bride. In this case, all faults are concealed and covered over and only the virtues are seen."

Despair of Grace the Greatest Sin

May 18, 1532

"The sin which Judas committed when he betrayed Christ was a small sin because it could be forgiven. But to despair of grace is a greater sin because it cannot be forgiven, for God has determined for Christ's sake to forgive the sin of those who believe. This sin is so great and wicked that it leads either to despair or to presumption. Consequently, one ought to be disposed to say, 'It is true. I have sinned. But I will not despair on this account or commit the sin again.' However, it's a calumny to conclude from these words of mine that it is permissible to sin and then to believe, for one can't believe in Christ unless one declares and resolves not to sin again. Sin carries us down to despair or up to presumption. In either case the sin is not repented of, for sin is either exaggerated or not acknowledged at all."

Dog Provides Example of Concentration

May 18, 1532

When Luther's puppy happened to be at the table, looked for a morsel from his master, and watched with open mouth and motionless eyes, he [Martin Luther] said, "Oh, if I could only pray the way this dog watches the meat! All his thoughts are concentrated on the piece of meat. Otherwise he has no thought, wish, or hope...."

A Lie Is Like a Snowball

Summer or Fall, 1532

"A lie is like a snowball. The longer it is rolled on the ground the larger it becomes."

Prayer and the Promise of God

Fall, 1532

"When we pray, we have the advantage [of the promise] that what we ask will be granted, although not according to our wish. If it weren't for the promise I wouldn't pray. God does well, moreover, that he doesn't give us everything as we wish, for otherwise we'd want to have everything on our own terms. That our Lord God is the same in life and death I have often experienced. If our prayer is earnest it will be heard, even if not as and when we wish. This must be so or our faith is vain. Consequently, it's difficult to pray. I know well what a prayer requires of me. I haven't committed adultery, but I've broken the first table[3] against God's Word and honor. On account of my great sins [against the first table] I can't get to the others in the second table."

It Is Easier to Doubt Than to Believe

November 8, 1532

A question was proposed by Master Ignatius, a student of sacred literature, on the day before the Kalends of December 1532: Why do we more readily believe Satan when he terrifies than Christ when he consoles? The question was answered by Dr. Martin Luther: "Because we are better equipped to doubt than to hope; because hope comes from the Spirit of God but despair comes from our own spirit. Accordingly, God has forbidden it [despair] under severe penalty.

---

3. I.e., the first table of the Decalogue, or the first three commandments.

That we more easily believe penalty than reward is a product of the reason or spirit of man. Hoping and believing are different from thinking and speculating. Reason sees death before it, and it's impossible for reason not to be terrified by it. Likewise, we can't be persuaded [by our reason] that God gives his Son and loves us so much, and hence we say, 'You have not allowed your Son to be crucified for nothing!' This is above reason. That God is so merciful, not on account of my works but on account of his Son, is incomprehensible.

"In this article, all the sect leaders are wanting, even if they say they believe it. I think they all have a bad conscience, and I point out in proof of this that when they are up against it they become desperate. . . . I hold, therefore, that they know they are wrong. Even so, the bishop of Mainz, the margrave, and Duke George make a joke of the Word of God, as Adam also did in paradise and as nature always does. When a man sins, he says it isn't important. But from this sin he proceeds to the sin against the Holy Spirit, and God lets him fall into willful sin. So, Duke George fell into sin, and he recognizes that he's doing wrong, but not only doesn't he refrain from sin but he doesn't ask to be forgiven. This is the sin against the Holy Spirit, and here one passes from the second to the first table [of the law]. When you feel that something is wrong and you have a bad conscience about it, this is not the sin against the Holy Spirit, but when you sin and have a good conscience about it, this is the sin against the Holy Spirit. . . .

"Dear Lord God, it is enough to have sinned without trying to justify oneself. This isn't tolerated in a home. The father of a household doesn't allow it. It burns in one's heart if a person who sins tries to justify himself. When you confess a sin and yet do not cease from it, it is a grievous sin and is contempt of God, but it's not the sin against the Holy Spirit. On the other hand, when you know you are wrong and nevertheless try to defend yourself, this is too much.

"Our Lord God can suffer it that no sin should be so great that it may not be forgiven when the sinner falls down before Christ. But Duke George relies on being forgiven by the Christian church, and so he goes on sinning, but he'll find out otherwise. One should have no doubt about a penitent sinner, even if he repeats his sin again and again, but one should also consider that if he dies in his sin he has had it.

"I think many of the kings of Israel, like Ahab, have been saved. About Solomon I have no doubt. So, we see that all history presses toward the forgiveness of sins. Everything circles around the center, and that is Christ."

There Are Two Kinds of Offense

December, 1532

"Offense is of two kinds, received and given. [An example of] offense received is that the Jews were offended by Christ because he spoke and acted according to the Word of God, just as God wished. This opinion needed to be uprooted. The pope is also offended because I teach Christian liberty, but what do I care? In fact, I preach against him so that it may be known that the doctrine of the papists is corrupt, but what I say and do is according to God. We belabor them, but for their own good, as Paul says.[4] I wish to offend them, not for their ruin but for their good. To defend error would be of the devil. If our Lord God lets a man fall so far that he doesn't think the Word is the Word, we don't wish to hold him but will let him go."

The Relation of Word, Spirit, and Faith

December, 1532

"Faith and the Spirit go together, but the Spirit is not always revealed. So, Cornelius had the Holy Spirit before Peter came to him, although he didn't know it.[5] Those in the book of Acts who said, 'We don't know the Holy Spirit,' also had the Spirit, just as the patriarchs in the Old Testament had Christ, although they didn't know him. They clung to the Word, and through it they received the Holy Spirit. Later in the book of Acts he was manifested to them outwardly. It is to be understood thus: The Word comes first, and with the Word the Spirit breathes upon my heart so that I believe. Then

---

4. Cf. Rom 10:19.
5. Cf. Acts 10:1–48.

I feel that I have become a different person and I recognize that the Holy Spirit is there. Accordingly, these are two things: to have the Holy Spirit and to know that you have him. When somebody speaks in your ear, you hardly hear his words before [you feel] his breath, so strong is the breath. Even so, when the Word is proclaimed, the Holy Spirit accompanies it and breathes upon your heart. The sophists[6] say that this is reflected knowledge, as an image is reflected in a mirror. When the Word is scattered abroad the Holy Spirit blows upon us, but he must also breathe upon us inwardly.

"Christ's saying concerning the Jews, 'They could not believe' [John 12:39], belongs in the box of secrets which it isn't given us to open. It's futile for anybody who is thus condemned to suppose that he would say to God, 'Why have you made me different?' For unbelievers will not come to the thought of asking, 'Why didn't you give me the Spirit?' But they will come to the thought, 'You had the law. Why didn't you keep it? You should have done so,' etc. Such thoughts will gnaw at them. They won't be able to think of anything else. They won't be able to get around their conscience. The greatest gift is to have a conscience pacified by the Word. For this did God permit his Son to die, that we might have a good conscience."

To Be Glad to Die Is Unnatural

December, 1532

"I don't like to see examples of joyful death. On the other hand, I like to see those who tremble and shake and grow pale when they face death and yet get through. It was so with the great saints; they were not glad to die. Fear is something natural because death is a punishment, and therefore something sad. According to the spirit one dies willingly, but according to the flesh the saying applies, 'Another will take you where you do not wish to go' [John 21:18]. In the Psalms and other histories, as in Jeremiah, one sees how eager men were to escape death. 'Beware,' Jeremiah said, or 'you will be bringing innocent blood upon yourselves' [Jer 26:15]. But when Christ said, 'Let this cup pass from me' [Matt 26:39], the meaning was dif-

---

6. Luther's usual term for the medieval scholastics.

ferent, for this was the Same who said, 'I have life and death in my hand' [John 5:21, 24]. We are the ones who drew the bloody sweat from him."[7]

Sunrise Suggests the Existence of God

Early in the year 1533

"That notion of the pope and of all the philosophers that if I am good I shall have a gracious God, and if not there is no God, means that one makes oneself into God. But I can't understand what must be in a man's mind if he doesn't feel seriously that there is a God when he sees the sun rise. It must at times occur to him that there are eternal things, or else he must push his face into the dirt like a sow. For it's incredible that they [the planets] be observed to move without inquiring whether there isn't somebody who moves them. In other areas, it's known that a house doesn't build itself, etc. . . ."

Erasmus Does Not Understand the Gospel

Early in the year 1533

"Paul calls it a mystery of God [Col 2:2] that Another bears our sin and says that he has committed it. Erasmus knows nothing about this. The Father says, 'What my Son promises you, I will do.' Only spiritual trial teaches what Christ is. I've often experienced how the name of Christ helps. God willing, nobody will drive me away from it. The Scriptures make me sure of this experience."

The Relation of Faith and Love in Paul

Early in the year 1533

"Concerning the verse in Galatians [5:6], 'faith working through love,' we also say that faith doesn't exist without works. However, Paul's view is this: Faith is active in love, that is, that faith justifies which expresses itself in acts. Now, it is assumed by some that the fruits of faith make the faith to be faith although Paul intends some-

---

7. Cf. Luke 22:44.

thing different, namely, that faith makes the fruit to be fruit. Faith comes first and then love follows. This also happens in the case of God's works. Circumcision, in so far as it is a work by itself, is of no account. But this, he says, is what counts: 'Believe in me and be godly.'"

Difference Between Samson and Julius Caesar

Spring, 1533

I asked what the difference was between Samson,[8] who had great strength, which he got from the Spirit, and Caius [Julius] Caesar[9] or some other man who was strong in body and mind. To this he [Martin Luther] replied, "The spirit of Samson was the Holy Spirit, who makes holy and who produces actions which are obedient to God and serve him. We can also speak of the Spirit among the heathen; that is, God also acts among them, but this is not sanctifying action. I often wonder about the example of Samson. There must have been a strong forgiveness of sins in his case. Human strength couldn't do what he did."

How to Deal with Thoughts that Trouble You

April 6, 1533

"When you are troubled by your thoughts, drive them away in any way you can—if not with some argument, then at least by conversation about something you find delight in."

When somebody objected that nothing great can be accomplished without weighty thoughts he [Martin Luther] replied, "Thoughts must be distinguished. Thoughts of the intellect do not make one sad, but considerations of the will do. They cause us to be vexed or pleased about something, and we have sad and melancholy thoughts when we sigh and complain. . . ."

---

8. Cf. Judges 14–16.
9. Julius Caesar, Roman general and ruler in the century before Christ.

Criterion for Worship Is Obedience, Not Beauty

Spring, 1533

"Hear and obey [Christ]! This is the greatest service of God. Nothing else counts. For do what we will, what God has in heaven is better and more beautiful than anything we can do. Otherwise Saul would have delighted him,[10] but God said, 'Your worship is only an annoyance,' although it was a beautiful service. Elsewhere it is written, 'Sacrifice and offering I have not desired, but I wish to be obeyed....'"[11]

Satan and a Christian Debate About Assurance

Spring, 1533

"Christ wished to humble Peter, for he wasn't content to ask once but asked again and again, 'Peter, do you love me? Feed my sheep[12] and lift them up without the severity of the law. Toward others, however, employ the severity of the law because they are not sheep, for I suffer and do all things for humble sheep.'

"In the light of nature and reason the highest wisdom is the law. When Satan speaks according to the law and says to you in your heart, 'God doesn't want to forgive you,' how will you as a sinner cheer yourself, especially if signs of wrath, like illness, etc., are added?

"[The devil says,] 'Behold, you are weak. How do you know, therefore, that God is gracious to you?' Then the Christian must come and say, 'I have been baptized, and by the sacrament I have been incorporated [in Christ]; moreover, I have the Word.'

"The devil objects: 'This is nothing, for many are called, but few are chosen' [Matt 22:14].

"Reply: 'They lose what they were baptized for. They don't accept it. They fall away again. They hold on to the law and forget Christ, therefore, they are not of the elect....'

"But a Christian remains firmly attached to Christ and says, 'If I'm not good, Peter wasn't either but Christ is good.' Such are the elect. Others say, 'God is gracious to me because I hope to mend my ways,'

---

10. Cf. 1 Sam 15:22.
11. Cf. Ps 40:6–8.
12. Cf. John 21:15–17.

but this is only a gallows repentance; the heart isn't in it. Although the wicked sometimes have compunctions (so they call them)—that is, promise themselves that they will be good—they soon depart from the straight path and seek to merit [a reward]. But a Christian says, 'I wish to do as much as I can, but Christ is the bishop of souls. To him will I cling, even if I sin.' It is thus that one has assurance."

Counsel for a Man Overtaken by Melancholy

Spring, 1533

I asked him [Martin Luther] about a certain man who, when he had a stomachache for several days and as a consequence had pain in his head and was confused in his thoughts, got the notion and was afraid that he was falling into a state of melancholy. He disclosed his anxiety to me and asked that I notify the doctor, whereupon he [Martin Luther] responded with these words: "When the devil can bring this about, it means that imagination has produced the effect. On this account, his thoughts ought to be changed. He ought to think about Christ. You should say to him, 'Christ lives. You have been baptized. God is not a God of sadness, death, etc., but the devil is. Christ is a God of joy, and so the Scriptures often say that we should rejoice, be glad, etc. This is Christ. Because you have a gracious God, he won't take you by the throat.'

"A Christian should and must be a cheerful person. If he isn't, the devil is tempting him. I have sometimes been grievously tempted while bathing in my garden, and then I have sung the hymn, 'Let us now praise Christ.' otherwise I would have been lost then and there. Accordingly, when you notice that you have some such thoughts, say, 'This isn't Christ.' To be sure, he can hear the name of Christ, but it's a lie because Christ says, 'Do not let your hearts be troubled [John 14:27]. Trust in me,' etc. This is a command of God: 'Rejoice!' I now preach this, and I also write it, but I haven't as yet learned it. But it happens that we learn as we're tempted. If we were always glad, the devil would befoul us. Christ knows that our hearts are troubled, and it is for this reason that he says and commands, 'Let not your hearts be troubled.' Thus, we are like the holy fathers in our faith. The weaker we are than the fathers, the greater the victory Christ obtains for us. We are very inexperienced, very weak, and very proud over against the devil; he has a great advantage over us, for our wisdom, power, and holiness are not so great as our fathers' were. But our Lord God wants to put an end to the devil's extreme arrogance. Paul had to say, 'I alone have resisted all the derision of Satan.'"

Devil Upsets Distinction Between Law and Gospel

Summer or Fall, 1533

"In a conflict with the devil it isn't enough to say, 'This is the Word of God,' for it is the devil's greatest [trick] to take away one's weapon when fear suddenly strikes. He has done this to me. He knows that in my heart I am constantly praying, 'Our Father,' etc., but he often harasses me about my not praying. The devil is the kind of spirit who won't leave the weapon in a person's hand if our Lord God steps out even for a moment. Accordingly, one must pray constantly, 'Father, help,' etc. Nobody should fight with the devil unless he first prays, 'Our Father.' It is a remarkable thing. He is hostile to us. We don't know a hundredth part of what he knows. He tempted Abraham, David, etc., and he knows how to get the upper hand. Judas was not tempted in his life, and so when his hour came he went ahead with self-assurance but without knowing what was before him.[13] We, who are at odds with the devil, know by God's grace how to resist him.

"It's the supreme art of the devil that he can make the law out of the gospel. If I can hold on to the distinction between law and gospel, I can say to him any and every time that he should kiss my backside. Even if I sinned I would say, 'Should I deny the gospel on this account?' It hasn't come to that yet. Once I debate about what I have done and left undone, I am finished. But if I reply on the basis of the gospel, 'The forgiveness of sins covers it all,' I have won. On the other hand, if the devil gets me involved in what I have done and left undone, he has won, unless God helps and says, 'Indeed! Even if you had not done anything, you would still have to be saved by forgiveness, for you have been baptized, communicated, etc.' But if I

---

13. Cf. Matt 26:47–50.

don't get this [help from God], it will be as it was in the case of Dr. Krause,[14] in Halle, who said, 'Alas, Christ accuses me.' There was the 'doing something.' If God had helped, he would have said, 'If you've done something, you've done it.' ('So, you are mine,' says the devil.) It hasn't come to that yet, for above 'doing' is 'believing.' But before one gets to believe, one is done for.

"So, don't be too daring. The distinction between law and gospel will do it. The devil turns the Word upside down. If one sticks to the law, one is lost. A good conscience won't set one free, but the distinction [between law and gospel] will. So, you should say, 'The Word is twofold, on the one hand terrifying and on the other hand comforting.' Here Satan objects, 'But God says you are damned because you don't keep the law.' I respond, 'God also says that I shall live.' His mercy is greater than sin, and life is stronger than death. Hence if I have left this or that undone, our Lord God will tread it under foot with his grace. But who can get so far in the present temptation? It was a bitter experience even for Christ himself[15] [and it would be for us], except that he has promised that he won't let us be tempted beyond our strength [1 Cor 10:13]. However, he often lets things go so far that one can't keep up."

Much Babbling Not Desirable for Real Prayer

Before December 14, 1531

"Our lay brothers in Erfurt had to pray four hundred Our Fathers in one day for the canonical hours. Once a certain brother said, 'If I were our Lord God I wouldn't like to hear what I alone must pray, to say nothing of having my ears filled with the babbling of all the brothers.' But when Moses cried out to God at the Red Sea[16] without using many words—that must have been a real prayer!"

---

14. When the Reformation had first been introduced in Halle, Saxony, John Krause, counselor of Archbishop Albrecht of Mainz, was inclined to favor it. Afterward he supported Albrecht in its suppression, whereupon he became troubled in conscience and committed suicide.
15. Cf. Matt 26:36–46. On the subject under discussion, see Thomas M. McDonough, *The Law and the Gospel in Luther* (Oxford: University Press, 1963).
16. Cf. Exod 14:15.

Luther Offers Spiritual Counsel to an Auditor

Between December 28 and 31, 1531

Then, after Master Philip had departed, he [Martin Luther] said to me, "Be of good cheer. Things will surely be better with you, for I know that your trials contribute to the glory of God and to your profit and that of many others. I, too, suffered from such trials, and at the time I had nobody to console me. When I complained about such spiritual assaults to my good Staupitz, he replied, 'I don't understand this; I know nothing about it.'

"You now have the advantage that you can come to me, to Philip [Melanchthon], or to Cordatus to seek comfort, and you must believe with confidence that we speak God's Word to you. If you plead for help from me, how much greater help will befall you from Christ when you plead for help from him who is a thousand times better than Philip or Cordatus? Just hold out! Let the devil rage! He will surely meet with a rebuff."

Thereupon, when I spoke to Dr. Luther about my temptations on the left and on the right hand, he replied, "The devil can do this in a masterful way; if he couldn't he wouldn't be the devil. The dear apostles were sinners, too, and were great big knaves, like Paul, who said, 'I formerly blasphemed and persecuted and insulted him; but I received mercy.' So, Peter betrayed him [Christ], which was a villainous trick. In short, Christ appointed the apostles for the forgiveness of sins, that in the apostles we may see the mercy of God in Christ. I believe that at times the prophets also played the fool. After all, they were human beings as much as we are."

Then I spoke about my temptation when I was approaching [the sacrament of] the altar. He responded, "Gerson and other fathers have said that one should adhere to one's original intention. It was your original intention to get forgiveness."

Not Solitude but Social Intercourse Advised

Between January 8 and March 23, 1532

"The papists and Anabaptists teach: If you wish to know Christ, try to be alone, don't associate with men, become a separatist.[17] This is plainly diabolical advice which is in conflict with the first and the second table [of the Decalogue]. The first table requires faith and fear [of God]. According to the second commandment, this is to be preached and publicly praised before men and is to be discussed among men. One must not flee into a corner. So, the second table teaches that one must do good to one's neighbor. We ought not to isolate ourselves but enter into companionship with our neighbor. Likewise, it [this notion] is in conflict with marriage, economic life, and political existence and is contrary to the life of Christ, who didn't choose solitude. Christ's life was very turbulent, for people were always moving about him. He was never alone, except when he prayed. Away with those who say, 'Be glad to be alone and your heart will be pure.'"

God May Be Known Only in Christ Jesus

May 20, 1532

At dinner on the day after Pentecost [Martin Luther said], "One shouldn't think of any other God than Christ; whoever doesn't speak through the mouth of Christ is not God. God wants to be heard through the Propitiator, and so he'll listen to nobody except through Christ. Though the Jews called and cried out, 'Lord, who livest; etc., they looked for God in many places, but not in the Propitiator, where he promised to hear them. So, it is in our case. Those who don't seek God or the Lord in Christ won't find him."

The Good Life of the Waldensians

Between December 11, 1532 and January 2, 1533

Luther commended the life of the Waldensians[18] as the most upright of all: "Outwardly they live very honorably. They keep their passions within bounds as much as possible. They're not arrogant. They attribute righteousness to others, for they don't claim to be

---

17. Luther probably had in mind the Nicolaitans, a gnostic sect of the second century.
18. The Waldensians (Waldenses), late medieval dissenters in Europe, owed their origin (ca. 1108) to Peter Waldo, a merchant in Lyons who had the Scriptures translated into the vernacular, advocated an ascetic life, and sharply criticized the priests of his day.

the only righteous persons. They reject the abomination of the mass, purgatory, the invocation of saints, etc. They have ministers of the Word who are celibate; these they permit to marry, but on condition that they give up their office. They don't condemn marriage and openly confess that they wouldn't shun married ministers if they couldn't have unmarried ones. This is the way it will be with us too; if we want to have ministers, we'll have to take burghers.

"Likewise, the Waldensians are not lazy or given to drunkenness. They have the best pedagogy. But they don't have the article of justification in its purity; they confess indeed that men are saved by faith and grace, but they understand faith as a quality that produces regeneration. They don't ascribe [everything] to faith alone in Christ. They explain faith and grace differently from us, and at the same time they attribute righteousness to works when they say, 'Faith apart from works is barren' [Jas 2:20]. If this passage is applied to morals and the preaching of the law, it is excellent, but if we connect it with the article of justification, it's not so much inappropriate as it is ungodly."

Trust in God or One's Own Goodness

Between January 26 and 29, 1533
"It's the Holy Spirit alone who attains to certainty of faith in Christ without any doubting. The adherents of the sects always utter some words from which their doubting spirit becomes manifest: 'I hope I'm godly,' 'I hope I'm righteous.' The Christian, on the other hand, says, 'I do what I can. What I don't get done the suffering of Christ will pay for me. I'm saved in Christ. Nobody shall take this confidence from me. Jesus is my Savior.' There's nothing else by which our God and our conscience may be put at rest. Those who put their trust not in Christ but in their own righteousness are always in doubt.

"When [as a monk] I had prayed, and said my mass, I was very presumptuous. I didn't see the scoundrel behind it all because I didn't put my trust in God but in my own righteousness, and I didn't thank God for the sacrament but expected him to thank me and be glad that

I had sacrificed his Son to him. We [monks] had a saying when we went to mass, 'I'll go and get the Virgin a child.'"

The Place of Reason in Christian Life

Between January 26 and 29, 1533

Dr. [Luther] was asked whether, since it is necessary to exclude reason from articles of faith, reason has any value at all for Christians. He replied, "Prior to faith and a knowledge of God, reason is darkness, but in believers it's an excellent instrument. Just as all gifts and instruments of nature are evil in godless men, so they are good in believers. Faith is now furthered by reason, speech, and eloquence, whereas these were only impediments prior to faith. Enlightened reason, taken captive by faith, receives life from faith, for it is slain and given life again. As our body will rise [from the dead] glorified, so our reason is different in believers than it was before, for it doesn't fight against faith but promotes it. Our speech, which used to be godless and blasphemous, now preaches, praises God, and gives him thanks. Thus, my speech is different from what it once was; now it's enlightened. So, iron which glows from fire is different from iron that doesn't glow. This is regeneration through the Word and occurs while the person and the members remain the same. . . .

"Reason, speech, and all gifts and created things are therefore different in believers and Christians than in unbelievers."

A Prayer for Rain in a Dry Season

June 9, 1532

It was a time of drought, and lifting up his eyes to heaven he [Martin Luther] said, "Lord God thou hast said through the lips of thy servant David, 'The Lord is near to all who call on him, to all who call on him in truth. He fulfils the desire of all who fear him, etc., and saves them' [Ps 145:18, 19]. How is it, then, that thou art unwilling to give us rain? If thou dost not give us rain, at least give us something better, like tranquility, life, and peace. But what will the ungodly say to these words, 'If you ask anything of the Father in my name [he will give it to you]' [John 16:23]? I know that we groan and cry unto thee from our hearts," etc.

That same night rain fell.

A Lesson Drawn from Timid Birds

June 9, 1532

When some birds built a nest in his garden and always flew away when we passed by, he [Martin Luther] said, "Dear little bird, don't fly away. I wish you nothing but good. If only you'd believe me! [Then he turned away from the nest and said,] This is how we should believe God—that he wishes us well with his whole heart. He who has given his Son for me certainly doesn't want to kill us."

The Nature of Pilgrimage Then and Now

Between March 28 and May 27, 1537

"In former times saints made many pilgrimages to Rome, Jerusalem, and Compostella[19] in order to make satisfaction for sins. Now, however, we can go on true pilgrimages in faith, namely, when we diligently read the psalms, prophets, gospels, etc. Rather than walk about holy places we can thus pause at our thoughts, examine our heart, and visit the real promised land and paradise of eternal life."

The Downcast Should Avoid Solitude

February 18, 1538

On February 18 Philip was very sad and downcast on account of the disobedience of his son-in-law, who would not permit his daughter to come to Wittenberg, although the mother and her children were to go to Halle in order to bring the daughter back for the father's consolation. This impudent disobedience of Sabinus so disturbed the father-in-law that he was inaccessible to any comfort and lived to himself, apart from the companionship of others. Luther pitied him and spoke at length with Dr. Cruciger, Zoch, and Milich

---

19. The tomb of St. James was alleged to be in Compostella (Santiago), Spain.

about Philip's wretchedness and melancholy and why it was that in his affliction he liked solitude when he ought rather to seek companionship.

"He is gnawing at his own heart," said Luther. "I, too, often suffer from severe trials and sorrows. At such times, I seek the fellowship of men, for the humblest maid has often comforted me. A man doesn't have control of himself when he is downcast and alone, even if he is well equipped with a knowledge of the Scriptures. It is not for nothing that Christ gathers his church around the Word and the sacraments and is unwilling to let these be hidden in a corner. Away with monks and hermits! These are inventions of Satan because they exist apart from all the godly ordinances and arrangements of God. According to the plan of creation every man is either a domestic or a political or an ecclesiastical person. Outside of these ordinances he is not a man, unless he is miraculously exempted. Accordingly, a solitary life should be avoided as much as possible."

Why God Places Christians in the World

August 31, 1538

"God placed his church in the midst of the world, among countless external activities and callings, not in order that Christians should become monks but so that they may live in fellowship and that our works and the exercises of our faith may become known among men. For human society, as Aristotle[20] said, is not an end in itself but a means [to an end]; and the ultimate end is to teach one another about God...."

An Exhortation to Die for Christ's Sake

March 16, 1539

On Laetare Sunday, March 16, he delivered a sermon and followed it with a very beautiful exhortation that we suffer death in Christ's name. "Although we are otherwise mortal on account of our sins, if we die in behalf of the Word of God our death will be very costly.

---

20. Greek philosopher (384–322 B.C.) who had great influence on medieval theology.

We'll all be saints, and our hide will be sold dearly enough. Not for our own sake would we pray for peace, therefore, since our death is gain, but for the sake of our posterity and the church of our descendants."

A Student Goes Home to See His Sick Father

May 7, 1539

Martin Weyer, a student of noble birth from Pomerania, was called back home by his father. Since the father was an old man and was accustomed to papistic usages, the son asked Dr. Martin Luther how he should deal with his father in order to be able to benefit him. He inquired if during the time of his father's illness he ought to attend papistic ceremonies and, in particular, private mass. Dr. Martin Luther replied that he should in every way accommodate himself to his father, under no circumstances offend him, and adapt himself to his fasting, praying, invocation of the saints, and hearing of masses. At the same time, Luther said, through the Word of God the son should instruct his parent in the doctrine of justification and the words of the Creed. Above all, he should diligently impress upon him the preaching of Jesus Christ, and only after all this should he dwell on his upright life and his pure conversation. Then there will be hope for the father. If the father should not be changed by all this, the son must bear his infirmity, pray, and commend him to God. He should take care in every possible way not to offend his father by his liberty but should become the spiritual father of him who is his physical father. If for this purpose, he adjusts himself to his father, he will not sin by attending mass and other profane rites.

Holiness in This and the Future Life

Between May 21 and June 11, 1540

Severus said, "Doctor, there is a certain doctor in Linz who is sorely tried because he cannot find perfect righteousness in himself and because, when he prays, blasphemies against Christ always come to his mind."

"This is a good sign," Luther replied. "There are two kinds of blasphemy. First, there is active blasphemy when we consciously and intentionally look for reasons to blaspheme. . . . God keep us from this! But, second, blasphemy is passive when the devil introduces such perverse thoughts into our heads against our will and in spite of our struggle against them. By means of these thoughts God wishes to occupy us so that we don't get lazy and snore but fight against them and pray. But when the end of life approaches, these temptations cease, for then the Holy Spirit is near to his Christians, keeps the devil at a distance, and gives us a tranquil and quiet mind.

"This happened to me in Gotha.[21] Being certain that I was about to die I said farewell to everybody, called Pomeranus, commended to him the church, the school, my wife, and the rest, and asked him to absolve me of my sins. . . . Thus, with a peaceful mind and without any struggle at all I would have fallen asleep in Christ. But Christ wished me to live on. So also, my Katy,[22] when we had all given up hope for her life, would have died willingly, happily, and with complete peace, and she said nothing at all but, 'In you, O Lord, I seek refuge; do not let me ever be put to shame' [Ps 31:1]. She repeated this more than a thousand times." She was now seated at the table and confirmed this. Then the doctor added, "If we hadn't had children I wouldn't have said one more prayer for her but would have committed her soul to Christ's keeping.

"Wherefore, Dr. Severus, you ought to write that man [in Linz] that he shouldn't torment himself but should have confidence. In his good time the devil will of his own accord stop forcing such blasphemies upon him. As far as perfect righteousness is concerned, I can readily believe that he desires to be perfectly righteous and that he tries to be holy and blameless. But such a life would be a life of angels and it will not be ours except in the future life. I often get angry with myself because I find much impurity in myself. But what should I do? I can't divest myself of my nature. Meanwhile Christ deems us righteous on account of his blood and counts for righteousness the fact

---

21. In 1537, after he had been taken ill in Smalcald and was returning to his home in Wittenberg, Luther had stopped in Gotha, where he had suffered a relapse.
22. The reference here is to the grave illness of Luther's wife a few months before.

that we desire to be righteous, abhor this uncleanness, and love his Word and trust in him.

"Surely as far as we and our princes are concerned, we are not pure and holy, and our princes have their faults. But Christ rejoices in a clear and trustful confession. Certainly, I esteem it highly. By saying one word and denying the Word our princes[23] could have returned to the favor of king and emperor and lived quietly. But they preferred to lose everything and put themselves, their family, and their land in temporal danger rather than forsake the confession. This is the thing that terrifies the emperor and the pope; it also attracts many of us and encourages more people to confess their faith. I'm a beggar. What can I lose when I have nothing? But they risk the loss of their reputation and their principalities for the name of Christ.

"Consequently, even if we are not perfectly holy, Christ will wash away our sins with his blood and, when we depart from this life, will make us altogether pure in the life to come. In the meantime, we are content with that righteousness which exists in hope through faith in Jesus Christ. Amen."

Christians as Sheep in the Midst of Wolves

Between May 21 and June 11, 1540

"Christ fights with the devil in a curious way—the devil with great numbers, cleverness, and steadfastness, and Christ with few people, with weakness, simplicity, and contempt—and yet Christ wins. So, he wished us to be sheep and our adversaries to be wolves.[24] But what an unequal contest to fight with ten or a hundred wolves! He sent twelve disciples into the world, twelve among so many wolves. I think it's a remarkable war and a strange fight in which the sheep are killed and the wolves stay alive. But they'll all go to ruin as a result, because God alone performs miracles. He'll preserve his sheep in the midst of the wolves and he'll crush the jaws of the wolves forever."

---

23. The allusion here is probably to the steadfastness of the evangelical princes, and especially of the elector of Saxony, at the imperial Diet of Augsburg in 1530, where the Augsburg Confession was presented.
24. Cf. Matt 10:16. Luther expressed similar thoughts in a letter to Philip Melanchthon on June 18, 1540.

We Do Not Believe that God Is Creator

September, 1542

Turning to Master Holstein he [Martin Luther] said, "Master, where were you sixty years ago? Where was I? Where did I come from? Certainly, we didn't make ourselves inasmuch as we were nothing. There must be someone who made us. And do we rashly propose to make a bargain with our Lord God to sell him our works, in return for which he is to give us heaven? Isn't it a disgraceful thing for a creature to dare to lift himself up so high and deal with his Creator in such a fashion? It's because we don't believe that God is the Creator. If we believed in him as the Creator we'd surely act differently. But nobody believes in him as the Creator, even if one says so and even if one's conscience convinces one that God is the Creator of all that is ours. If we had been created by another God, it might have made some sense if we approached God and said, 'Lord God, have regard for me on account of my works! I come to thee although thou hast not made me!'"

Wealth the Most Insignificant Gift of God

Winter of 1542–1543

"Riches are the most insignificant things on earth, the smallest gift that God can give a man. What are they in comparison with the Word of God? In fact, what are they in comparison even with physical endowments and beauty? What are they in comparison with gifts of the mind? And yet we act as if this were not so! The matter, form, effect, and goal of riches are worthless. That's why our Lord God generally gives riches to crude asses to whom he doesn't give anything else."

To Believe and to Comprehend Are Not the Same

Spring, 1543

When Dr. Jonas said that the mind of man cannot comprehend articles of faith and that it is enough that we begin only to assent, the doctor [Martin Luther] said, "Yes, dear Dr. Jonas, if one could believe them the way they're written, our hearts would leap for joy. That's certain. Accordingly, we won't arrive at the place where we comprehend them. In Torgau, a wretched little woman once came to me and said, 'Ah, dear Doctor, I have the idea that I'm lost and can't be saved because I can't believe.' Then I replied, 'Do you believe, dear lady, that what you pray in the Creed is true?' She answered with clasped hands, 'Oh yes, I believe it; it's most certainly true!' I replied, 'Then go in God's name, dear lady. You believe more and better than I do.'

"It's the devil who puts such ideas into people's heads and says, 'Ah, you must believe better. You must believe more. Your faith is not very strong and is insufficient.' In this way, he drives them to despair. We are so constructed by nature that we desire to have a conscious faith. We'd like to grasp it with our hands and shove it into our bosom, but this doesn't happen in this life. We can't comprehend it, but we ought to apprehend it. We should hold to the Word and let ourselves drag along in this way."

Everybody Must Believe for Himself

Spring, 1543

When he was asked whether somebody else's faith will secure salvation for a person, he [Martin Luther] replied, "By all means! In fact, the faith of one person may obtain another's whole conversion. Accordingly, it's said that Paul was converted and saved by Stephen's prayer.[25] However, Paul wasn't accepted on account of Stephen's faith, but Stephen's faith obtained faith for Paul from God and by this faith he was saved in God's sight. Many people have been preserved by prayer, as we prayed Philip back to life.[26] Ah, prayer accomplishes much."

Somebody else asked, "But, Doctor, wasn't Paul converted long after the death of Stephen?"

The doctor responded, "Not at all! He was converted that same year. He was still a fine, young man and was learned. He adhered to the righteousness of the law: 'By doing so one shall live' [Lev 18:5;

---

25. Cf. Acts 7:59–60.
26. When Philip Melanchthon was in Weimar in 1540, he was overtaken by a grave illness. Luther was convinced that his prayers brought his friend back from the edge of the grave.

Rom 10:5]. He thought he was pleasing God in this way. It's impossible that God shouldn't hear a prayer of faith. Whether he always does is another matter. God doesn't give according to the prescribed measure, but he presses it down and shakes it together, as he said [Luke 6:38].

"This is what Augustine's mother did. She prayed to God that her son might be converted. But nothing seemed to help. She approached all sorts of learned men and asked them to persuade her son. At length, she proposed to him that he marry a Christian girl in order that she might bring him back, but it didn't work. But when our Lord God came along he acted effectively and made such an Augustine out of him that he's now called an ornament of the church. So, James said well, 'Pray for one another,' etc., for 'the prayer of the righteous is powerful and effective' [Jas 5:16]. This is one of the best verses in that epistle. Prayer is a powerful thing, if only one believes in it, for God has attached and bound himself to it [by his promises]."

2

Table Talks on the Ministry

Impatience Is Not Necessarily a Sin

Between April 7 and 15, 1532

When I asked him about the passage in which Jeremiah cursed the day on which he had been born[1] and suggested that such impatience was a sin, he [Martin Luther] replied, "Sometimes one has to wake up our Lord God with such words. Otherwise he doesn't hear. It is a case of real murmuring on the part of Jeremiah. Christ spoke in this way, 'How much longer must I put up with you?' [Mark 9:19]. Moses went so far as to throw his keys at our Lord God's feet[2] when he asked, 'Did I conceive all this people?' [Num 11:12]. It can't be otherwise. It's annoying when one has the best of intentions but things don't turn out well. Surely this is murmuring. I do the same, and I can't banish the thought from my mind when I wish that I had never started [this business].[3] So likewise when I wish I were dead rather than witness such contempt [for the Word of God and his faithful servants]. Accordingly, it is only speculative theologians who con-

---

1. Cf. Jer 20:14.
2. I.e., give up his job.
3. I.e., the Reformation.

demn such impatience and recommend patience. If they get down to the realm of practice, they will be aware of this. Cases of this kind are exceedingly important. One should not dispute about them in a speculative way.

"It is a great thing to set a true preacher in motion, and unless our Lord God himself gets him going, nothing will come of it. It requires a mighty spirit to serve people in body and soul and yet suffer extreme peril and the basest ingratitude for so serving. [Jesus] therefore asked Peter, 'Do you love me?' and then said, 'Feed my lambs' [John 21:15]. It is as if he would say, 'If you wish to be a true pastor, only the love with which you love me will do. Otherwise it is impossible, for who will suffer ingratitude and give up money and health to study, only to expose himself to the gravest danger?' Therefore, he says, 'It is necessary that you love me.'"

A Preacher Should Vary His Style

Between April 7 and 15, 1532

"A preacher is like a carpenter. His tool is the Word of God. Because the materials on which he works vary, he ought not always pursue the same course when he preaches. For the sake of the variety of his auditors he should sometimes console, sometimes frighten, sometimes scold, sometimes soothe," etc.

Office and Person Must Be Distinguished

Summer or Fall, 1532

"One ought to think as follows about ministers. The office does not belong to Judas but to Christ alone. When Christ said to Judas, 'Go, baptize,' Christ was himself the baptizer and not Judas because the command comes from above even if it passes down through a stinking pipe. Nothing is taken from the office on account of the unworthiness of a minister. So, when the prefect distributes grain in the name of our prince, the people get the whole grain despite the fact that the prefect is an adulterer.[4] Office and person must be distinguished. It is even so in the case of alms which I give through a thief, etc.

"Thus, the pope has a true ministry, although he abuses it. He does not abolish the Word, baptism, or the sacrament [of the altar] but only misuses them. Accordingly, the sacraments ought to be received from them [the papists], except for the sacrament of the altar, which they still corrupt. The Jews did not repudiate Moses, either, although they distorted him. Christ therefore said, 'Hear them!'[5] Nor does the pope forbid the Word but desires that it be understood as he understands it. He does not abolish the Word but only misuses it. The issue is use and abuse. To take a crude example, if somebody proposed to put on a crown like a pair of breeches, we would say that the crown ought to be placed on the head. It is not the thing that is rejected but the proper use of it. The thing is perverted. Instead of grasping a knife by the handle, it is grasped by the cutting blade. This is not what the spiritualists[6] do; they throw the knife away altogether and say that it is no knife. So, the Anabaptists reject baptism almost entirely. The pope, who distorts it, nevertheless allows baptism to remain. The spiritualists take away the substance; the pope takes away only the accident.

"Likewise, it is the true name of God that is used wrongly, for unless the godless misused the true name, why was it necessary to prohibit this? Therefore, anybody who misuses the name of God misuses the true name of God, as it is said, 'You have blasphemed my name,' and yet those who misuse God's name do not take the name away, but the name remains. So, the pope can also misuse a sacrament, and yet true baptism and the true sacrament [of the altar] remain. Otherwise how could the pope sin unless he had the true name of God and the true sacraments? Even so, the seditious man sins against the magistrate and yet does not remove the magistrate himself. For the pope has the Word and the sacraments not for himself but because he is in the public ministry, and consequently those who hear him hear the true Word of God. So, Judas says, 'Rise up

---

4. The town prefect in Wittenberg was Hans Metzsch, taken to task often by Luther for his profligate life.
5. Cf. Luke 16:29.
6. German: *Schwermer, Schwärmer*. Literally, 'swarmers,' i.e., enthusiasts, fanatics, or spiritualists.

in the name of Jesus Christ,' but he doesn't believe a word of it. The pope also baptizes. The pope occupies an office, and that's where you Bohemian Brethren and we get our office too."

Comfort When Offenses Arise over Teaching

Early in the year 1533

"Offenses arise from my teaching, but I comfort myself as Paul did when he wrote to Titus that this truth was revealed to further the faith of the elect [Titus 1:1]. For the sake of the elect it [the deed of Christ] was done. It is for their sake that we preach, for they are serious about it. I wouldn't lose a word over the rest. I've bitten into many a nut, believing it to be good, only to find it wormy. Zwingli and Erasmus are nothing but wormy nuts that taste like crap in one's mouth."

The Trials of a Preacher and Reformer

Early in the year 1533

"If I were to write about the burdens of the preacher as I have experienced them and as I know them, I would scare everybody off. For a good preacher must be committed to this, that nothing is dearer to him than Christ and the life to come, and that when this life is gone Christ will say to all, 'Come to me, son. [You have been my dear and faithful servant].'[7] I hope that on the last day he'll speak to me, too, in this way, for here he speaks to me in a very unfriendly way. I bear [the hatred of] the whole world, the emperor, and the pope, but since I got into this I must stand my ground and say, 'It's right.' Afterward the devil also speaks to me about this, and he has often tormented me with this argument, 'You haven't been called,' as if I had not been made a doctor."[8]

---

7. Cf. Matt 25:21.
8. Luther often appealed to his doctor's degree as the ground for his authority to instruct and reform the church.

What Is Involved in a Call to the Ministry

Spring, 1533

"First of all, this is certain: young people must be brought up to learn the Scriptures. Later they will know that they are to be educated to be pastors. Afterward they will offer their services when some position is unoccupied. That is to say, they will not force their way in but will indicate that they are prepared, in case anybody should ask for them; thus, they will know whether they should go. . . . To force one's way in is to push somebody else out. But to offer one's service is to say, 'I'll be glad to accept if you can use me in this place.' If he is wanted, it is a true call. So, Isaiah said, 'Here am I; send me!' [Isa 6:8]. He went when he heard that a preacher was needed. This ought to be done.

"A young man should find out whether somebody is wanted, and then whether he is wanted. The latter must also be. What is to be said about talents is touched upon in the text that speaks about servants who are called.[9] It is written in Paul, 'Whoever aspires to the office of bishop desires a noble task' [1 Tim 3:1]. . . ."

How to Preach on the Annunciation of Mary

March 25, 1533

On the festival of the Annunciation of Mary in 1533 he [Martin Luther] said, "When preaching on this day one should stick to the story, so that we may celebrate the incarnation of Christ, rejoice that we were made his brethren, and be glad that he who fills heaven and earth is in the womb of the maiden. Disputations stand in the way of joy because they bring forth doubts, and these produce sorrow, just as if the girl had not rejoiced until she knew that she was promised in marriage and her doubt vanished. Therefore, I hate Erasmus from the bottom of my heart because he calls into question what ought to be our joy. Bernard[10] filled a whole sermon with praise of the Virgin Mary and in so doing forgot to mention what happened. . . .

---

9. Cf. Luke 19:12–27.
10. Bernard of Clairvaux *(ca.* 1091–1153).

But a Christian puts the questions aside and occupies himself with the effects [of the incarnation]. The incarnation, therefore, should be held high. Mary can't be sufficiently praised as a creature, but that the Creator himself comes to us and becomes our ransom—this is the reason for our rejoicing. I don't think the story can be told more simply than it was by Luke. Nobody could have invented the word 'sent.'"[11]

Christ Taught Only in a Corner of Judaea

Spring, 1533

"The authority of Christ when he taught wasn't so great as ours is today. He himself said, 'Greater works than these will you do' [John 14:12]. He is the grain of mustard seed, but we are the bushes [Matt 13:31, 32]. Accordingly, he said, 'They were unwilling to bear me, although I taught in a comer, but you must bear me throughout all the world.' To preach Christ is to offend the flesh, but to preach the flesh is to offend Christ."

It Is God's Way to Speak Through Others

Spring, 1533

"At the time of Balaam there were true preachers and there were false. Where the text states that he would first go away and consult God [Num 23:3], this is to be understood as meaning that he would consult true preachers and that these advised him not to do it.[12] Then Moses explained himself by saying that Balaam no longer went to the right persons (as before).[13] . . . Accordingly, this expression (namely, that he consulted God) indicates to us that those people esteemed the Word of God highly because they had regard for what was said and not for who was speaking. So, it was said of Rebekah[14] that she did not inquire of God but of Shem or some other patriarch. For God always had certain persons and places in the world. He sent Moses,

---

11. Cf. Luke 1:26.
12. An early variant reads: 'not to undertake anything against God.'
13. Cf. Num 24:1.
14. Cf. Gen 25:22.

and when Moses said something they had to concede, 'Not Moses, but God has spoken.'

"After Moses God sent Christ. His teaching is also certain and his person is sure, and so we are not mistaken in concluding, when we hear something from him, that it is God who has said it. For he said from heaven, 'This is my Son, listen to him' [Matt 17:5]. Afterward, when Christ went away, he sent apostles and instituted sacraments (baptism and the Lord's Supper), so that when these are present and are heard and received we can truly say, 'God says this.' Often when I was troubled by something, Pomeranus or Philip or even my Katy would speak to me, and I was comforted as I realized that God was saying this because a brother was saying it either out of duty or out of love. For God says that we should listen to Christ, but Christ says that we should listen to the apostles.

"This leads the sacramentarians[15] astray. They speak according to their own ideas, but we speak what God says. Before the world existed, God said, 'Let there be a world,' and the world was.[16] So, he says here [in the Lord's Supper], 'Let this be my body,' and it is, nor is it prevented by the scoffing of Bullinger, who says that because the body of Christ isn't seen it isn't present. For in the former instance God created visible things but in the latter instance he created invisible, in such fashion as he wished."

Authority of Minister Resides in Office, Not Person

Spring, 1533

"From the passage, 'Receive the Holy Spirit. If you forgive,' etc. [John 20:22, 23], some conclude that therefore only those who personally have the Holy Spirit are able to forgive sins. But this isn't the meaning, for Christ gives the Spirit to the public office and not to a private person, as he had just said, 'As the Father has sent me, so I send you' [John 20:21]." Consequently, he was speaking about those who

---

15. Luther's favorite term for those (especially Anabaptists and Zwinglians) who denied that the sacraments are means of grace. Luther put on the right those who are today generally placed on the left. Cf. Roland H. Bainton, *Studies on the Reformation, Collected Papers* (Boston: Beacon Press, 1963), pp. 119, 120.
16. Cf. Gen 1:1–31.

had been called and who had the authority to preach, administer the sacraments, etc. When somebody has the authority to preach he also has the authority to administer the sacraments, for we hold that the sacrament is less important than preaching. . . .

Human Frailty in the Face of God's Demands

Summer or Fall, 1533

"God makes fools of both theologians and princes, for he commits to us an impossible task which nobody would undertake if he knew about it beforehand but which he is not allowed to relinquish once it has been committed and undertaken. So, it is with the rest of our work. We demand many things, but they aren't done except to a limited degree. We teach many things, but they are learned only to a modest extent. 'Nothing is successful,' as the preacher of Solomon says [Eccles 1:1, 2].

"Why does God act so? Because he alone is wise and powerful. Because if our suggestions and ideas were carried out we would become presumptuous and would claim wisdom and power for ourselves. Because we surround the glory of wisdom and power with the defects which belong to our nature. We want to set things straight and make everything right. To this God says, 'Well, then, go ahead! Be clever and do a good job! Be a preacher and make the people godly! Be a lord and mend the people's ways! Get to it at once!'

"What a retrogression would occur! And the conclusion would be: 'Vanity of vanities' and 'Let wisdom be attributed to God alone' [Eccles 1:2; 2:26]. We are fools and wretched bunglers in all we do and attempt."

A Question About Making the Miracles Known

Fall, 1533

When I asked, with reference to the passage[17] whether those sinned who had been forbidden by Christ to say anything and nevertheless made the miracles public, he [Martin Luther] replied, "When

---

17. Cf. Mark 1:44.

Christ spoke outside of his office he spoke as God, but when he spoke according to his office he spoke as a man and a servant. When he spoke about his person outside of his office he said, 'All that the Father has is mine' [John 16:15], 'Believe in God, believe also in me' [John 14:1]. But when he spoke according to his office and not about his person, he said, 'I have come to serve' [Matt 20:28]. Thus, it is according to his office that he forbids making the miracles public. Therefore, they did well to preach the miracles which he showed them, and he also did well to prohibit this. This is evident from the fact that the evangelist boasts about them. In the whole gospel [of John] one can see that Christ wishes to glorify not himself but the Father. He [John] wrote this as an example for us preachers."

A Sermon Should Be Relevant to Its Hearers

Between January 8 and March 23, 1532

"One should preach about things that are suited to a given place and given persons. A preacher once preached that it's wicked for a woman to have a wet nurse for her child, and he devoted his whole sermon to a treatment of this matter although he had nothing but poor spinning women in his parish to whom such an admonition didn't apply. Similar was the preacher who gave an exhortation in praise of marriage when he preached to some aged women in an infirmary."

How to Go About the Task of Preaching

Between May 20 and 27, 1532

He [Martin Luther] said to Anthony Lauterbach, "When you are to preach, speak with God and say, 'Dear Lord God, I wish to preach in thine honor. I wish to speak about thee, glorify thee, praise thy name. Although I can't do this well of myself, I pray that thou mayest make it good.' When you preach, don't look at Philip or Pomeranus or me or any other learned man, but think of yourself as the most learned man when you are speaking from the pulpit.

"I have never been troubled by my inability to preach well, but I have often been alarmed and frightened to think that I was obliged to speak thus in God's presence about his mighty majesty and divine nature. So be of good courage and pray."

Some Suggestion Concerning Preaching

Between June 12 and July 12, 1532

"In my preaching I take pains to treat a verse [of the Scriptures], to stick to it, and so to instruct the people that they can say, 'That's what the sermon was about.'

"When Christ preached, he proceeded quickly to a parable and spoke about sheep, shepherds, wolves, vineyards, fig trees, seeds, fields, plowing. The poor lay people were able to comprehend these things."

The Long Sermons of John Bugenhagen

January 26, 1533

"Every high priest should have his private sacrifices. Accordingly, Pomeranus sacrifices his hearers with his long sermons, for we are his victims. And today he sacrificed us in a singular manner."

God Governs His World Through Frail People

Between October 27 and December 4, 1536

"It is remarkable that God has committed to us preachers the ministry of the Word for the ruling of people's hearts, which we can't look into. But this is the office of God, who says to us, 'Preach! I shall give the increase I know the hearts of people.' This should be our comfort, even when the world laughs at our office...."

The Preacher and the Notes of His Sermon

Between October 27 and December 4, 1536

"Our Lord God wishes himself to be the preacher, for preachers often go astray in their notes so that they can't go on with what they have begun. It has often happened to me that my best outline came undone. On the other hand, when I was least prepared my words flowed during the sermon...."

Then Martin Luther said, "Oh, it isn't like a lawsuit. But many are casual and careless and pay no heed to what and how they preach. Dr. Pomeranus is sufficiently full and solid in his sermons. On the other hand, I am thin and dry. When I hear Pomeranus, he gives me many commonplaces on which my thoughts may roam, and therefore he is a very good preacher."

Martin Luther said that he is often troubled in his sleep by the suggestion that he has to preach but doesn't have an outline.

Preach to the Simple and Not to the Learned

Between March 28 and May 27, 1537

Rector Bernard von Dolen, minister in Herzberg, complained bitterly about his arrogant auditors who despised the reading of the catechism. Dr. Martin [Luther] was greatly disturbed and fell silent. Then he said, "Cursed be every preacher who aims at lofty topics in the church, looking for his own glory and selfishly desiring to please one individual or another. When I preach here I adapt myself to the circumstances of the common people. I don't look at the doctors and masters, of whom scarcely forty are present, but at the hundred or the thousand young people and children. It's to them that I preach, to them that I devote myself, for they, too, need to understand. If the others don't want to listen they can leave. Therefore, my dear Bernard, take pains to be simple and direct; don't consider those who claim to be learned but be a preacher to unschooled youth and sucklings."

Large Churches Unsuitable for Preaching

February 26, 1538

Afterward there was mention of large churches which are not suited to preaching. "Cologne has a cathedral [Martin Luther said] that is so large that it has four rows of columns, each row consisting of twenty columns. These are extraordinary buildings, but they aren't

39

suitable for listening to sermons. Good, modest churches with low arches are the best for preachers and for listeners, for the ultimate object of these buildings is not the bellowing and bawling of choristers but the Word of God and its proclamation. The cathedral of St. Peter in Rome and the cathedrals in Cologne and Ulm are very large but inappropriate."

Difference Between Apostles and Bishops

May 21, 1538

"The papists boast that their authority in the church goes beyond the Word, and they use this argument: The apostles changed baptism, and therefore the bishops are permitted to change the sacraments.

"The papists should be given this answer: Supposing the apostles did make some changes, there is nevertheless a great difference between an apostle and a bishop. An apostle is a person who is ordained by God immediately and called with gifts of the Holy Spirit, but a bishop is a person chosen by men for the preaching of the Word and the ordination of ministers in a certain place. Accordingly, the apostles had authority, but this is not granted to bishops. So, Elijah killed false prophets,[18] but similar power is not accorded to any pastor at all. Paul therefore makes a clear distinction: His gifts were that some should be apostles, some doctors, some pastors.[19]

"Among the apostles there was no primacy, but equality. And the apostle is a universal person, above a bishop. However, the definition of the superiority of Peter over the bishops is false because the definition extends beyond what is defined, for the conclusion is drawn that the pope is the supreme authority for ordaining ministers, assembling relics, and transferring kingdoms. We don't concede this definition, for any good definition ought to be framed distinctly, properly, plainly in order that neither more nor less is comprehended in the definition than in that which is defined."

---

18. Cf. 1 Kings 18:40.
19. Cf. Eph 4:11.

Danger of Future Schism in the Church

June 27, 1538

Luther and Melanchthon had supper together in the former's home after a deposition.[20] They spoke at length and sorrowfully about future times, when there would be many teachers. "There will be great confusion [said Luther]. Nobody will conform with another man's opinions or submit to his authority. Everybody will want to be his own rabbi and the greatest offenses and divisions will arise from this. It would have been best, therefore, if the princes had prevented this by holding some sort of council. But the papists avoid a council, so much do they fear the light."

Thereupon Master Philip responded sadly, "The pope will never be persuaded to have a general council. He proceeds against us only with guile and force."

[Luther observed:] "It's said that Nicholas von Schonberg, bishop of Capua, admonished the pope with the best reasons that he should deal honestly with the issue before the church, make some concessions to the Germans, and not fulminate against them with his authority. The Germans, he said, are men who won't yield in a just and honorable cause, nor can they be overcome with guile or with force. But the pope ridiculed the godly counsel of this man. Would that our princes and estates might call a council and establish some measure of agreement in doctrine and ceremonies in order that everybody who wishes to do so might not burst forth rashly to the scandal of many! This is already beginning to happen. Truly the image of the church is deplorable! The church lies hidden under very great weakness and offense."

News About Preaching the Gospel in Italy

July 1, 1538

On July 1, news arrived in writing from Italy that recently in Bologna forty-two monks preached the gospel in public with free-

---

20. Deposition was the name given to the ceremonial initiation to which older students subjected students who were entering the university.

dom and clarity, that they spoke with as much boldness as it could have been done in Wittenberg, and that their numerous auditors received them with great applause, and yet the bishops and the pope resorted to force against them. When advised to flee, they took care of themselves, but one of them, who had books by Luther and books in translation under the name of Erasmus of Rotterdam, was seized and imprisoned while the books were burned. Master Philip said, "The Word of God doesn't fall into empty space but spreads from here into every land. If it reaches Italy it will be clung to tenaciously, for Italians are persevering, not fickle or inconstant."

One Should Stop Preaching When Finished

July 7, 1538

"The Gospel for the Third Sunday after Trinity is an excellent portrait," said Luther, "of how God is disposed toward sinners and of how solicitously he seeks them out. The subject and theme of this gospel is repentance, for it speaks of contrite and penitent sinners, to whom this gospel should be preached."

Thereupon he asked Master Cyriacus, "Did you exhaust this text when you preached yesterday?"

"Yes, indeed," he replied, "I emptied my bag of all that was in it."

To this Luther said, "Then it was time to stop, for I have learned this art: When I have nothing more to say I stop talking." Then he told the story of a certain monk who was a beginner as a preacher. "When he had practiced his sermon, and had memorized eight pages of manuscript, he delivered it rapidly word for word. In a quarter of an hour he was finished with the sermon. His bag was empty. Dear God, men like this who knew nothing were supposed to have been rectors of the churches!"

Contempt for Word and Shortage of Ministers

September 10, 1538

It was said in Lochau that six hundred of the richest parishes in the diocese of Würzburg are vacant. He [Luther] commented, "This will have bad consequences. It will happen among us, too, if contempt for the Word and its ministers continues to be so great. If I wanted to get rich under these circumstances I wouldn't preach but would be a juggler and travel about the country. For the sake of money I'd have plenty of spectators.

When the visitors[21] reproached the farmers, and inquired why they were unwilling to support their parish ministers when they were providing livings for their cattle herders, the farmers replied, 'Because we can't get along without a herder.' For shame, that it has come to this in my lifetime! The antinomians[22] contribute a great deal to this. They increase the presumption among secure people, and I now see so much presumption in the antinomians that under the covering of trust in [God's] mercy they dare to do whatever they please, as if the believer no longer sins and as if believers are so righteous that they don't need any preaching of the law. They dream of a church as righteous as Adam was in paradise, though the wrath of God was revealed from heaven against him[23] when God said, 'Adam, you may eat of every fruit but if you eat of this tree you shall die.'"[24]

Two Kinds of Sinners, Penitent and Secure

November 16, 1538

"To distinguish between two kinds of sinners, the penitent and the secure, is especially necessary for the preacher, otherwise all Scripture remains closed. Consequently, at the beginning of the sermon which he preached before numerous princes in Smalcald, Amsdorf said sharply, 'The gospel belongs to the poor and afflicted and not to you princes and lords who live in luxury, without tribulations.' It was an ill-humored introduction calculated to win favor! Yet it had to be, because this most spiritual teaching of the gospel disturbs even the best and most godly people. We see in the Pauline epistles with what zeal Paul opposes them: 'Put to death, therefore, whatever in you is

---

21. Since 1528, clergymen and lawyers had been appointed by the elector of Saxony to make visits of inspection to all parishes. According to a later report of the same incident, the farmers spoke not to the visitors but to Luther himself.
22. The antinomians claimed that believers were free of the law.
23. Cf. Rom 1:18.
24. Cf. Gen 2:16.

earthly' [Col 3:5]. 'If, in our effort to be justified in Christ, we ourselves have been found to be sinners . . .' [Gal 2:17]. One sees that it's not only the law that makes hypocrites; the disturbing thing is that even the doctrine of grace should make hypocrites. This distinction between two kinds of sinners must therefore be held on to and must be followed by excommunication. My 'No' means as much as your 'Yes.'"

The Quibbling of Sophists to Be Avoided

November 17, 1538

"The world must be considered carefully [Martin Luther said]. It's governed by opinions, and therefore it's ruled by sophistical hypocrisy and tyranny. True religion is compelled to serve them as a maidservant. One must therefore be careful and beware of sophistry, which consists not only of equivocation in words but flourishes under all circumstances, so that in religion it possesses a magnificent pretense under the guise of Holy Scripture. There's more harm in sophistry than any person can perceive; our nature, which is prone to lying, can't see the evil in sophistry at all. Plato[25] offers a remarkable description of sophistry: People who can twist everything, repudiate the opinions of others, and draw conclusions on both sides . . . are not to be praised. These are sly tricks. It's the glory of a good character [on the other hand] to seek the truth and to rejoice in guilelessness."

The Hatred Between Laymen and Clergymen

November 25, 1538

On November 25, there was discussion of the perpetual hatred between clergymen and laymen. "This is not without reason Luther said] because untamed people don't want to be corrected, but it is the function of preachers to accuse them. This is an extremely burdensome and dangerous business, and therefore laymen counter by keeping a sharp eye on clergymen. They have to find some fault with

---

25. In his *Gorgias,* Plato attacked the rhetoric of contemporary sophists and declared that it is better to suffer injustice than do it.

them and see some boils, even if they're only on the wives and children of the clergymen. In this way, the laymen try to get revenge. If the princes didn't have power over them, the people would pursue them with the same hatred. Only let us abide by the pure Word in order that we may sit on Moses' seat.[26] If life is not so well rounded and perfect, God will have mercy, even if the hatred of the laity should remain according to the old saying, 'When the ocean dries up and Satan is lifted up to the stars, the layman will be the trusted friend of the clergyman.'"

Preaching Should Be Simple, Not Erudite

Between May 21 and June 11, 1540

"Many sects will still arise and Osiander will start one of them, for that fellow can do nothing but criticize others. We translated the Bible, and he took up one and another word with which to attack us. These words and the whole quarrel don't really matter to Christendom, and he doesn't prove anything anyhow. He offends the church. He could have taken up and debated this matter in private, but he couldn't contain himself and curb his cleverness.

"In Smalcald I preached on a text from the Epistles of John.[27] in which it's stated that Christ dwells in us through faith and grace, works in us, and defends and saves us. Just as I fell ill[28] he [Osiander] rebuked me openly, though not by name, in the presence of all the learned men. Christ, he said, dwells in us essentially, etc. Everybody was annoyed by this. . . . Osiander possesses eloquence, follows an outline, and adheres to rules of rhetoric, but he doesn't instruct the people. On the other hand, Dr. Link and Master Veit instruct them. Today Master Morlin pleased me very much [when he preached]. He instructed the common people about the duties of wives and maidservants. A wife, he said, should think that she's in a holy estate and that her husband is a gift of God; a maidservant should also think that her estate is holy and that her work is holy. The people can take this

---

26. Cf. Matt 23:2.
27. In February, 1537, Luther preached at a meeting of the Smalcald League on 1 John 4.
28. Luther had a severe attack of kidney stones.

home with them, but nobody understands a sermon that is turgid, deep, removed from life.

"I spoke about this to Bucer in Gotha and suggested that he and Osiander should refrain from erudite preaching. Philip doesn't need to be instructed, and I don't teach or lecture for his sake, but we preach publicly for the sake of plain people. Christ could have taught in a profound way but he wished to deliver his message with the utmost simplicity in order that the common people might understand. Good God, there are sixteen-year-old girls, women, old men, and farmers in church, and they don't understand lofty matters! If one can present fitting and familiar comparisons, as Link can do in masterful fashion, the people will understand and remember. Accordingly, he's the best preacher who can teach in a plain, childlike, popular, and simple way. I prefer to preach in an easy and comprehensible fashion, but when it comes to academic disputations watch me in the university; there I'll make it sharp enough for anybody and will reply, no matter how complicated he wants to be. Someday I'll have to write a book against artful preachers."

How to Preach in Three Brief Steps

Between August 7 and 21, 1540

Conrad Cordatus said to Dr. Martin Luther, "Reverend Father, teach me in a brief way how to preach."

Luther responded briefly, "First, you must learn to go up to the pulpit. Second, you must know that you should stay there for a time. Third, you must learn to get down again."

He added nothing in addition to these words, and as a result Cordatus was quite angry. Yet at length it occurred to him that the doctor had hit the mark very well. Anybody who keeps this order will be a good preacher. First, he must learn to go up to the pulpit, that is, he should have a regular and a divine call. Second, he must learn to stay there for a time, that is, he should have the pure and genuine doctrine. Third, he must also learn to get down again, that is, he should preach not more than an hour (which didn't please Pomeranus).

It Is Christ who Absolves, Not the Minister

Between August 7 and 24, 1540

"This ought especially to be taught, that confession is not made to the minister but to Christ. Likewise, it isn't the minister who absolves but Christ. But few understand this. Today I replied to the Bohemians, who insist that God alone remits sins and are offended by my little book on the keys. Wherefore one should teach that people make confession to Christ, and Christ absolves through the mouth of the minister, for the minister's mouth is the mouth of Christ and the minister's ear is the ear of Christ. It's to the Word and the command that one should pay attention, not to the person. Christ sits there, Christ listens, Christ answers, not a minister."

The Term "Word" Has Various Meanings

Between August 7 and 24, 1540

Somebody asked, "Doctor, is the Word that Christ spoke when he was on earth the same in fact and in effect as the Word preached by a minister?"

The doctor [Martin Luther] replied, "Yes, because he said, 'Whoever listens to you listens to me' [Luke 10:16]. And Paul calls the Word 'the power of God' [Rom 1:16]."

Then the inquirer asked, "Doctor, isn't there a difference between the Word that became flesh [John 1:14] and the Word that is proclaimed by Christ or by a minister?"

"By all means!" he replied. "The former is the incarnate Word, who was true God from the beginning, and the latter is the Word that's proclaimed. The former Word is in substance God; the latter Word is in its effect the power of God, but isn't God in substance, for it has a man's nature, whether it's spoken by Christ or by a minister."

Some Preachers Are Much Too Voluble

Between September 2 and 17, 1540

"When Morlin, Medler, or Master Jacob preach it's as if one pulled the bung out of a full barrel. Out it flows as long as there's something in the barrel. Such fluency of speech doesn't benefit the auditors, even if it gives pleasure to some people, nor does it instruct. Accordingly, it's better to speak clearly. Thus, the hearer can take hold of something."

A Usurer Should Be Excommunicated

Between September 2 and 17, 1540

The doctor [Martin Luther] said, "Manifest usurers should be excommunicated, that is, they should not be given the sacrament, as I did in the case of the nobleman."

Thereupon somebody asked, "What if he's penitent?"

The doctor replied, "There's a limit to everything. However, he must become a Zacchaeus[29] and return what he stole in excessive interest to those out of whom he sweated it. Otherwise he's not truly repentant. According to civil law, not to speak of divine law, he can't with a good conscience keep this money anyhow. Whoever eats and drinks with him makes himself a participant in his sins. Consequently you, Master Mickell, should never eat with him."

Should One Preach Law or Gospel More?

Between September 18 and 23, 1540

"Doctor, many men think and say that the law should be emphasized often for the sake of the profane common people, lest they abuse the gospel. Others say that the common man ought not to be cited as a reason but only the command of Christ, who wishes that the goodness of the Father may become known through the gospel. Which of these opinions is the better?"

The doctor [Martin Luther] replied, "This shouldn't and can't be comprehended in a fixed rule. Christ himself preached [the law and the gospel] according to his circumstances. As a passage or text indicates, therefore, one should take up the law and the gospel, for one must have both. It isn't right to draw everything into the gospel

---

29. Cf. Luke 19:2–10.

alone; nor is it good always to preach the law alone. The Scriptures themselves, if properly adhered to, will give the answer."

A Preacher Should Not Say Everything at Once

Summer or Fall, 1542

When Katy said that she could understand the preaching of her husband's assistant Polner better than that of Pomeranus because the latter wandered too far from his subject, the doctor [Martin Luther] responded, "Pomeranus preaches the way you women usually talk. He says whatever comes to mind. Dr. Jonas is accustomed to say, 'One shouldn't hail every soldier one meets.' And it's true, Pomeranus often takes everybody he meets along with him. Only a fool thinks he should say everything that occurs to him. A preacher should see to it that he sticks to the subject and performs his task in such a way that people understand what he says. Preachers who try to say everything that occurs to them remind me of the maidservant who is on her way to market. When she meets another maid, she stops to chat with her for a while. Then she meets another maid and talks with her. She does the same with a third and a fourth and so gets to market very slowly. This is what preachers do who wander too far from their subject. They try to say everything all at once, but it won't do."

Gross Sinners Excommunicate Themselves

Summer or Fall, 1542

"Our usurers, gluttons, drunkards, whoremongers, blasphemers, and scoffers shouldn't be excommunicated by us. They excommunicate themselves. They despise the Word of God, enter no church, hear no sermon, receive no sacrament. If they don't want to be Christians, let them be heathen, and forever! Who cares about this anyhow? If they take the goods of ministers and appropriate everything for themselves, the minister shouldn't absolve them or administer the sacrament to them. They shouldn't be allowed to attend any baptism, any honorable wedding, or any funeral. They should behave among us as heathen, which they'll be glad to do! When they are dying, no minister or chaplain should visit them, and when they have died the hangman should drag them outside the town to the carrion pit, and no student or chaplain should escort them. If they want to be heathen we'll treat them as heathen," etc.

3

Table Talks on the Word of God

What It Takes to Understand the Scriptures

Fall, 1531

"I wonder whether Peter, Paul, Moses, and all the saints fully and thoroughly understood a single word of God so that they had nothing more to learn from it, for the understanding of God is beyond measure.[1] To be sure, the saints understood the Word of God and could also speak about it, but their practice did not keep pace with it. Here one forever remains a learner. The scholastics illustrated this with a ball which only at one point touches the table on which it rests, although the whole weight of the ball is supported by the table.

"Though I am a great doctor, I haven't yet progressed beyond the instruction of children in the Ten Commandments, the Creed, and the Lord's Prayer. I still learn and pray these every day with my Hans and my little Lena. Who understands in all of its ramifications even the opening words,[2] 'Our Father who art in heaven'? For if I understood these words in faith—that the God who holds heaven and earth in his hand is my Father—I would conclude that therefore I am lord of

---

1. Cf. Ps 147:5.
2. Of the Lord's Prayer. Cf. Matt 6:9.

heaven and earth, therefore Christ is my brother, therefore all things are mine, Gabriel is my servant, Raphael is my coachman, and all the other angels are ministering spirits[3] sent forth by my Father in heaven to serve me in all my necessities, lest I strike my foot against a stone. In order that this faith should not remain untested, my Father comes along and allows me to be thrown into prison or to be drowned in water. Then it will finally become apparent how well we understand these words. Our faith wavers. Our weakness gives rise to the question, 'Who knows if it is true?' So, this one word 'your' or 'our' is the most difficult of all in the whole Scripture. It's like the word 'your' in the first commandment, 'I am the Lord your God' [Exod 20:2]."

The Order of the Ten Commandments

Early November, 1531

"The first to the seventh commandments follow one another in good order. Murder is a graver sin than adultery, adultery is a graver sin than stealing, etc. The order of the other three commandments is not so apparent. Although I do not presume to make a judgment, it is my opinion that the last three commandments speak, as it were, of the ground or circumstances of the preceding commandments, for it is with the mouth and with coveting (these are the two things that are forbidden in the last three commandments) that one sins against all the other commandments. The order certainly appears to shift in the eighth commandment, for to bear false witness is not a graver sin than to covet your neighbor's wife, nor is it a graver sin to covet your neighbor's house than his wife."

Contempt for and Love of God's Word

Between November 9 and 30, 1531

When there was talk about contempt for the Word of God among peasants, noblemen, and townspeople, he [Martin Luther] said, "Such contempt ought to be both a consolation and a warning to us, so that we give thanks to God for the blessing of being among those

---

3. Cf. Heb 1:14.

who love his Word, diligently hear and learn God's Word, and find delight in the Holy Scriptures. For it is a great punishment and a severe judgment of God if a man so hates God and his Word that he is unwilling to hear it and neither honors nor esteems the ministers of the Word."

"Are You the Only One Who Is Right?"

Between November 30 and December 14, 1531

"Above all, we must be certain that this [our] teaching is the Word of God. When this is established, we shall be sure that the cause must and will remain and that no devil can suppress it. God be praised, I am certain that it is the Word of our Lord God. I have driven from my heart all other beliefs in the world, whatever they may be, and I have almost overcome that most difficult of all thoughts which arises in the heart, 'Do you claim to be the only one who has the true Word of God and no one else has it?' In this sense—that is, in the name of the church—they are now attacking us most severely. I find this argument [of our opponents] everywhere in all the prophets, to whom men said, 'We are the people of God; you are only a few.' Only in such a way should one rely upon oneself and say, 'All the rest of you are wrong.' But a consolation is added when the Word declares, 'I shall give you children, people who will accept it.'"[4]

Nobody Knows Distinction Between Law and Gospel

Before December 14, 1531

"There's no man living on earth who knows how to distinguish between the law and the gospel. We may think we understand it when we are listening to a sermon, but we're far from it. Only the Holy Spirit knows this. Even the man Christ was so wanting in understanding when he was in the vineyard that an angel had to console him [John 12:27–29]; though he was a doctor from heaven he was strengthened by the angel. Because I've been writing so much and so long about it, you'd think I'd know the distinction, but when a

---

4. Cf. Isa 54:13; Matt 13:8.

crisis comes I recognize very well that I am far, far from understanding. So, God alone should and must be our holy master."

A Comparison of Proverbs and Ecclesiasticus

Summer, 1532
"In Proverbs, the eighth chapter is the best. Similar to this is the first chapter of Ecclesiasticus. In both, however, there is nothing about Christ, nor are there promises or prophecies. Therefore, the Psalter, Isaiah, Jeremiah, and even Daniel are far superior to the books of Solomon as far as prophecies are concerned. Those are the best books in the Bible which, like Daniel, devour the Turks and treat of the kingdoms of the world. So, in neither [Proverbs nor Ecclesiasticus] is there anything about Christ or about promises or about the kingdoms of the world or about future events, but only about rules of life."

Now, then, the question is raised: Which of the two teaches better about rules of life and is superior to the other? "They have nothing theological except about wisdom, that is, about the Word of God, whence he is called wise who has the Word of God."

Two Rules for Translating the Bible

Summer or Fall, 1532
"In translating the Holy Scriptures, I follow two rules:
"First, if some passage is obscure I consider whether it treats of grace or of law, whether wrath or the forgiveness of sin [is contained in it], and with which of these it agrees better. By this procedure, I have often understood the most obscure passages. Either the law or the gospel has made them meaningful, for God divides his teaching into law and gospel. The law, moreover, has to do either with civil government or with economic life or with the church. The church is above the earth in heaven, where there is no further division but only a mathematical point, and so principles cannot fail there. This is (and Gerson[5] said it is supreme wisdom) to reduce all things to the first principle, that is, to the most general genus. In theology, there are law

---

5. Jean Gerson (1363–1429), learned French scholar to whose works Luther often appealed.

and gospel, and it must be one or the other. Gerson calls this reduction to the most general genus. So, every prophet either threatens and teaches, terrifies and judges things, or makes a promise. Everything ends with this, and it means that God is your gracious Lord. This is my first rule in translation.

"The second rule is that if the meaning is ambiguous I ask those who have a better knowledge of the language than I have whether the Hebrew words can bear this or that sense which seems to me to be especially fitting. And that is most fitting which is closest to the argument of the book. The Jews go astray so often in the Scriptures because they do not know the [true] contents of the books. But if one knows the contents, that sense ought to be chosen which is nearest to them."

Many Things Not Recorded in Scripture

October, 1532

"Moses wrote nothing about the creation of angels, first, because he wrote only about the creation of visible things and, second, because he didn't wish to give occasion for speculation. Our Lord God did well to leave many things unwritten. Besides, we would have belittled what we now have and would have sought after the things that are higher."

Luther Abandoned Early Allegorization

Summer or Fall, 1532

"When I was a monk I was a master in the use of allegories. I allegorized everything. Afterward, through the Epistle to the Romans, I came to some knowledge of Christ. I recognized then that allegories are nothing, that it's not what Christ signifies but what Christ is that counts. Before I allegorized everything, even a chamber pot, but afterward I reflected on the histories and thought how difficult it must have been for Gideon to fight with his enemies in the manner reported.[6] If I had been there I would have befouled my breeches for

---

6. Cf. Judg 7:1–23.

fear. It was not allegory, but it was the Spirit and faith that inflicted such havoc on the enemy with only three hundred men. . . ."

Translation of the Psalms and the Prophets

Between January 8 and March 23, 1532

"By God's grace the Psalter and the Prophets have now been completed in a good translation[7] so that we might get more from the bare text than from long commentaries. Hence, I don't like my Psalter,[8] for it is made up of a great deal of idle chatter. I used to be so fluent that I almost talked the whole world to death. I couldn't do this now. I have changed my mind about it. There was a time when I could ramble on at greater length about a little flower than I can now about a large field. I don't like verbosity."

Jonas said in response, "It's from the Holy Spirit and it pleases me."

First Words of Genesis Hard to Understand

June 8 or 9, 1532

In the evening [Martin Luther said] in the garden, "Before a man learns the first words in Moses, 'God created the heavens and the earth' [Gen 1:1], he is dead. Even if he lived to be a thousand years old, he wouldn't understand them fully. The Creator was so completely forgotten that God had to send his Son into the world to remind the world of the Father's benefaction and grace in the creation and in the sending of his Son," etc.

The World Becomes Weary of the Word of God

Between July 12 and August 12, 1532

"The world has now become very sure of itself. It relies on books and thinks that if these are read it knows everything. The devil almost succeeded in getting me, too, to become lazy and secure and to think:

---

7. A revised translation of the Psalter was published in the spring of 1531, and the following year all the prophetical books of the Old Testament appeared together. The conversation of Luther here recorded probably occurred while the latter work was on the press.
8. The reference may be to Luther's extensive commentary on the Psalms published in 1515.

'Here you have the books. If you read them you'll have the answers.' So, the fanatics and sacramentarians suppose that because they have read only one little book they know everything. Against such security, I pray the catechism[9] every day like my little Hans and ask God to keep me in his dear, holy Word, lest I grow weary of it."

Luther Reads Through Bible Twice a Year

October 21, 1532

"For some years now," the doctor said, "I have read through the Bible twice every year. If you picture the Bible to be a mighty tree and every word a little branch, I have shaken every one of these branches because I wanted to know what it was and what it meant."

We Do Not Make God's Word True or Untrue

Between June 9 and 12, 1532

"The objectivity and certainty of the Word remain even if it isn't believed. Everything depends on one's having the true sacrament of the altar, likewise true baptism, and also on my preaching the true Word of God. I stake my soul on it and am ready to die for it. If you believe without doubting, you'll be saved; if not, you'll be damned. I put my confidence in no other faith, but in the Word of God.

"Let me give an example. If I gave you one hundred florins and hid them from you under the table and you believed and said that they were merely lead or a lead alloy, what difference would that make to me, who offered you gold? It's your fault that you don't believe. The gold's gold, even if you don't think so. God doesn't lie when he promises eternal life. Only let us be sure that we appropriate it for ourselves in faith. For our unbelief doesn't make God's promise empty. On the contrary, poverty is the companion of truth."

---

9. The traditional parts of the catechism that were taken up in Luther's *Small Catechism:* The Ten Commandments, Apostles' Creed, and Lord's Prayer.

Sacramentarians Stress Spirit Without Word

Spring, 1533

"The devil has no better way to conquer us than by leading us away from the Word and to the Spirit. I have observed this as something remarkable in the sacramentarians that they don't consider the Word but only the things added to the Word, namely, the bread and wine. But one should hold fast to the Word and not concede the Spirit to people apart from the Word. The sacramentarians see only bread and wine (and, in like manner, water) but not the Word. So, they see only the serpent held up on a pole in Numbers 21 [:4–9], and not the Word."

There Are Many Things We Do Not Know

May 12, 1533

Master Philip examined a student in Anthony Lauterbach's home. He was a schoolmaster in Stargard, and when he answered thoughtlessly Philip said, "Do not answer so abruptly and burst out so heedlessly, for there are more things we do not know than there are things we know."

Luther remarked in connection with this, "Jonas once claimed that he knew everything in the Holy Scriptures and was angry at me because I didn't let this claim pass unnoticed. But I know there are many things I don't know. I have preached for twenty-five years and still don't understand the verse, 'The one who is righteous will live by faith' [Rom 1:17]."

Interpretation of the Betrayal of Christ by Judas

Summer or Fall, 1533

"I wonder that nothing is written [in the Scriptures] about Judas' knavery against Christ.[10] I think he did this mostly with his tongue, as Christ complained about him in the psalm [41:6–9]. He must have gone to the Pharisees and spoken crossly about Christ, saying, 'I bap-

---

10. Cf. Matt 26:47–50; John 13:21–30; 18:2–5.

tize, too, but I see it's different,' etc. He was also a thief[11] and hoped to get a large sum from Christ. . . . Judas must also have been a wicked man, because it is never without cause that the man [Jesus Christ] is as hostile to anybody as he was in Psalm 41. He must have laid in wait for Jesus. Otherwise, if he hadn't been so wicked, our Lord God would have forgiven him, as he did Peter, who also fell;[12] but it was on account of weakness that Peter couldn't stand."

There Is Much to Be Learned from Judas

Summer or Fall, 1533

"Judas is as important in the company of the apostles as any other three of the apostles, and he throws light on countless arguments, like the article of justification against the Donatists, who said that one could baptize only those who had the Holy Spirit. There are many proofs that Judas was an apostle, that is, one of the Twelve. Accordingly, what he did in his office was right, but when he was a thief he sinned. One must distinguish him from his office, for Christ did not commit theft to him but an office.

"Judas also throws light on the reproach that is heaped on us: 'There are many wicked people among you.' Very well! And Judas was an apostle! Undoubtedly, he behaved better than the others; nobody charged him with making any mistakes at table. Judas was really the pope, therefore, for the pope also snatched the money box.[13] He appeared to confess Christ, but actually he had nothing but the name [of Christian]. . . ."

Questions Put to Luther to Answer

August 19, 1538

In a letter [which arrived] on August 19, Master Forster set before Luther several questions that troubled him.

First, he asked whether preachers should criticize publicly, although the fraternal rebuke referred to in Matthew 18 [:15] seems

---

11. Cf. John 12:6.
12. Cf. Matt 26:69–75, John 18:15–18, 25–27.
13. Cf. John 13:29.

to speak only of personal sins. Should not those who have sinned openly by their teaching be rebuked openly, as Moses did to Korah, Dathan, and Abiram,[14] as Elijah did to the Baalites,[15] as Paul did to Peter,[16] and as we publicly opposed the pope? Luther replied, "A brother ought first to be rebuked privately, especially if the fault is new and involves only a few people. But if the error is firmly rooted among many people, so that it's not possible to approach every individual and admonish him separately, the error must be rebuked and refuted publicly."

The second question: The texts in Numbers 35 [:6] and Deuteronomy 19 [:3] seem to permit private revenge to a person who lays hold of the manslayer of a relative before he betakes himself to a city of refuge. These passages appear to be in conflict with the Scripture that forbids private revenge.[17] He [Luther] replied, "That precept in Moses is judicial and is abrogated, just as the usury of the Jews was permitted among the Gentiles and only ceased when other judicial decisions were made."

The third question: Why did Ruth act according to the law of propinquity when Boaz wasn't the brother of her deceased husband[18] and the law in Deuteronomy 25 [:5] clearly stipulates the brother of the deceased husband? He [Luther] replied, "This passage is an exposition of the law in Deuteronomy 25 [:5], namely, that if the brother of the deceased man is unwilling, then the next to him in blood kinship should marry her. Besides, Ruth didn't demand that Boaz marry her, but he did so because he had had an intimate connection with her when she couldn't be seen by him very well. I have treated this text in the English disputation."[19]

The fourth question: [What may be said] to the Judaizers, who demand testimonies from the Old Testament, namely, that Mary was

---

14. Cf. Num 16:1–40.
15. Cf. 1 Kings 18:17–46.
16. Cf. Gal 2:11.
17. Cf. Rom 12:19.
18. Cf. Ruth 3:1–4, 17.
19. In the fall of 1535, and the spring of 1536, a series of discussions was held in Wittenberg between representatives of King Henry VIII of England, headed by Bishop Fox of Hereford, and Luther and his colleagues. While not the main subject under discussion, the question of the king's divorce was introduced in the 'English disputation' here alluded to.

of the tribe of Judah and belonged to the house of David, when it is plain that the tribes and families were scattered after the Babylonian exile? He [Luther] replied, "Our evangelist expressly states that Mary was of the tribe of Judah.[20] Those who don't want to believe this may remain infidels. Moreover, such Judaizers can't find support for themselves in the last chapter of Judges,[21] where the tribe of Benjamin was disrupted. On account of fornication this tribe was not an honorable people of God, but it was separated and excommunicated from the people of God, and accordingly six hundred of them were compelled to take as their wives Gentiles and women who were carried off."

The fifth question concerned the passage of the Scriptures in Joshua 24 [:19], "You cannot serve the Lord, for he is a holy God. He is a jealous God; he will not forgive your transgressions or your sins." It seems plain that in these words an ungodly people is rejected, yet immediately after these words we read, "If you forsake the Lord and serve foreign gods" [Josh 24:20]. These words refer to those who had hitherto been godly and had not yet fallen away. Luther replied, "This was the farewell speech of Joshua. He admonishes the people with extraordinary feeling, as if he would say, 'I fear that you will provoke God's wrath again. If so, God will punish you, for he can't tolerate this. If you provoke him and fall away from him, God will be angry,' etc. Another solution is that the earlier words were said of the ungodly and the later words of the godly, just as we have many psalms in which, here and there, people are praised and are lifted up to heaven and immediately after are put down into hell; by synecdoche, in the former case the godly in the whole people are spoken of, and in the latter case the ungodly. We do the same thing in our churches when we preach; we praise those among the people who are good and then, on the other hand, we reprove the bad and the ungodly. So, the church is called holy, although only the smallest part of it is actually holy."

The sixth question: Whether a married man, whose wife was caught in adultery or whose wife left him, can marry another woman while the first is still living? Does not a second wedding seem to be

---

20. Cf. Matt 2:6.
21. Cf. Judg 21:1–24.

fornication or adultery instead of marriage? He [Luther] replied, "In 1 Corinthians 7 [:15] Paul expressly declares that second marriage is permitted when he says, 'But if the unbelieving partner desires to separate, let it be so; in such a case the brother or sister is not bound. For God has called us to peace,' etc. It's evident that this passage allows remarriage...." Then Luther told of a case in Eisenach, where a wife was unwilling to cohabit with her husband and repeatedly left him without cause. "At length," he said, "we permitted the husband to marry another woman but forbade the guilty party [to marry again]."

The seventh question: When Balaam took counsel so often with a spirit and received different answers,[22] was it the true God whom he consulted, and did he get his answers from the true God? He [Luther] replied, "He should have clung to the Word. But after a time, his greed, stirred up by Balak's promises, turned his attention to sorcerers, who spoke otherwise. The third time the true God again resisted him through the angel, but afterward he turned his attention to the sorcerers; and although the text reads that God met Balaam [Num 23:4], as if the Lord replied, nevertheless the voices were imitated and not the real thing. It's like the papists, who glory in the true God and Christ and yet under his name glory in and do the works of the devil. On this the text is clear."

The eighth question: How is one to understand the passage in Joshua 5 [:9], where it reads, "The Lord said to Joshua, "Today I have rolled away from you the disgrace of Egypt."? He [Luther] replied, "The answer is easy, for after Moses had circumcised the people according to the law, he said, 'Now you are no longer Egyptians; now that you are circumcised you are no longer heathen.'"

The ninth question: Did David sin when he offered to fight against the people of God in the presence of Achish?[23] He [Luther] replied, "He didn't sin because Saul was then a reprobate and was no longer king of God's people; he was in the place now occupied by the papists. In the second place, David didn't offer his service voluntarily but because he was under the Philistines. He was summoned as a

---

22. Cf. Numbers 22 and 23.
23. Cf. 1 Sam 29:8.

minister by the king, just as our subjects can fight against the church of the papists.

The tenth question: How is the passage in 1 Samuel 2 [:25] to be understood, "If one person sins against another, someone can intercede for the sinner with the Lord; but if someone sins against the Lord, who can make intercession?" He [Luther] replied, "It's more tolerable to sin against the second table [of the Decalogue] than against the first. Let him just examine the Decalogue and he'll see that a sin against the first table is greater than a sin against the second."

The eleventh question: Could Saul prophesy by the evil spirit, and if so, what was the prophecy like? He [Luther] replied, "At the time that he prophesied Saul didn't act by the evil spirit. Moreover, his prophecy was an exposition of the law in his home."

The Word Must Be Rightly Divided

October 7, 1538

"The Word of God should be rightly divided, and with care, for people are of two kinds. On the one hand are the contrite, who need consolation. On the other hand, are the rigid ones, to whom apply the law, threats, examples of wrath, the fire of Elijah,[24] the waters of the flood, and the destruction of Jerusalem; these must be attacked at once and must be made to feel terror."

Obedience or Opposition to the Word of God

November 20, 1538

Thereupon he [Martin Luther] spoke of the very great folly of all people which consists of this, that we wretched ones wish to make judgments concerning the Word of God, which we ought rather give ear to. "It's as if a vessel tried to teach the potter how to make it," he said, "how many fingers to use in shaping it.[25] Even so we wish to set ourselves up against God, we wretched creatures against our Creator. It is written, 'Listen to him' [Matt 17:5], and 'Hear, O daughter,

---

24. Cf. 1 Kings 18:20–40.
25. Cf. Rom 9:20, 21.

consider, and incline your ear; forget your people and your father's house' [Ps 45:10].

"Yes, even if Adam had not fallen, we would nevertheless have accommodated ourselves to the Word alone. Are we now, in a particular situation and in darkness, to despise that Word? The great folly of the pope's church is that it's based only on the external rule of reason, without the Word of God, and our salvation is supposed to be bound up with outward child's play. If this had only had to do with moral and legal matters!"

Absolution Is a Form of the Word of God

Between February 22 and 25, 1539

Then he [Martin Luther] spoke about the efficacy of the Word of God and about the joy in the church when brethren comfort one another with the Word of God. "There's something great about the employment of the keys and of private absolution when the conscience can be put to rest. Consequently, I'm unwilling to discard absolution. For under the papacy I was always a despairing monk, even when I made the greatest efforts. Finally, I received comfort from a brother through this one Word. God himself has commanded us to hope. Our salvation is faith in God. Why shouldn't we trust in God, who bids and commands us to hope? Through this Word he gave me life again."

The Authorship of Ancient Writings

Between May 21 and June 11, 1540

"Genesis is the right book. One should read and learn it. There we see that the ancient patriarchs agree with our faith. In my opinion, however, Genesis was not by Moses, for there were books before his time and books are cited—for example, the Book of the Wars of the Lord and the Book of Jashar.[26] I believe that Adam wrote for several generations, and after him Noah and the rest, to describe what happened to them. For the Jews were writers in very ancient times. The

---

26. Cf. Num 21:14; Josh 10:13.

Greeks started late, and the Germans have been writing for barely a thousand years."

The Study of the Bible Demands Humility

Between May 21 and June 11, 1540

"The Holy Scriptures require a humble reader who shows reverence and fear toward the Word of God and constantly says, 'Teach me, teach me, teach me!' The Spirit resists the proud. Though they study diligently and some preach Christ purely for a time, nevertheless God excludes them from the church if they're proud. Wherefore every proud person is a heretic, if not actually, then potentially. However, it's difficult for a man who has excellent gifts not to be arrogant. Those whom God adorns with great gifts he plunges into the most severe trials in order that they may learn that they're nothing. Paul got a thorn in the flesh to keep him from being haughty.[27] And if Philip[28] were not so afflicted he would have curious notions. When on the other hand, Jacob and Agricola[29] are haughty and despise their teachers and learning, I fear it may be done with them. . . . Pride drove the angel out of heaven and spoils many preachers. Accordingly, it's humility that's needed in the study of sacred literature."

From Allegorical to Literal Interpretation

Between October 3 and 19, 1540

The doctor [Martin Luther] said, "I can't work anymore, nor can I speak any longer. When I was young, I was learned, especially before I came to the study of theology. At that time, I dealt with allegories, tropologies, and analogies and did nothing but clever tricks with them.[30] If somebody had them today they'd be looked upon as

---

27. Cf. 2 Cor 12:7.
28. Philip Melanchthon's physical infirmities may have been in Luther's mind here.
29. John Agricola was Luther's chief antinomian opponent.
30. According to the fourfold method of biblical interpretation in the late Middle Ages, scholars sought various meanings in a text. In addition to the literal meaning there were believed to be other meanings: an allegorical (doctrinal), a tropological (moral), and an analogical (pertaining to the future) meaning.

rare relics. I know they're nothing but rubbish. Now I've let them go, and this is my last and best art, to translate the Scriptures in their plain sense. The literal sense does it—in it there's life, comfort, power, instruction, and skill. The other is tomfoolery, however brilliant the impression it makes."

Translating the Bible Meant Hard Work

Between October 19 and November 5, 1540
"Nobody believes what labor it cost us—except those who work with us and hear about it, like George.[31] For the rabbis help us very little. I plan to put a new preface in the front of the Bible to warn everybody about the rabbis, for they are blinded and hardened. Even if they already have the book, as Isaiah said [Isa 9:11–21], they are blind to it.

"This German Bible (this is not praise for myself but the work praises itself) is so good and precious that it's better than all other versions, Greek and Latin, and one can find more in it than in all commentaries, for we are removing impediments and difficulties so that other people may read in it without hindrance. I'm only concerned that there won't be much reading in the Bible, for people are very tired of it and nobody clamors for it anymore."

Luther Has Low Opinion of Epistle of James

Summer or Fall, 1542
"We should throw the Epistle of James out of this school,[32] for it doesn't amount to much. It contains not a syllable about Christ. Not once does it mention Christ, except at the beginning [Jas 1:1; 2:1]. I maintain that some Jew wrote it who probably heard about Christian people but never encountered any. Since he heard that Christians place great weight on faith in Christ, he thought, 'Wait a moment! I'll oppose them and urge works alone.' This he did. He wrote not

---

31. George Rorer, deacon in Wittenberg, helped Luther with the revision of the German Bible, the 1541 edition of which was in preparation at this time. The intended preface to the whole Bible was not published.
32. I.e., out of the university in Wittenberg.

a word about the suffering and resurrection of Christ, although this is what all the apostles preached about. Besides, there's no order or method in the epistle. Now he discusses clothing and then he writes about wrath and is constantly shifting from one to the other. He presents a comparison: 'For just as the body without the spirit is dead, so faith without works is also dead' [Jas 2:26]. O Mary, mother of God! What a terrible comparison that is! James compares faith with the body when he should rather have compared faith with the soul! The ancients recognized this, too, and therefore they didn't acknowledge this letter as one of the catholic epistles."[33]

Where the Word Is, There Is Contempt

Winter of 1542–1543

"When the Word comes, contempt for it is there too. This is certain. One can see it in the case of the Jews. God sent them the prophets Isaiah, Jeremiah, Amos, etc., sent them Christ himself, even divided the Holy Spirit among the apostles, who cried out together, 'Be penitent!' But nothing helped. They all had to endure much. Soon Jerusalem lay in ruin, and it remains so to this day. The same thing will happen in Germany. I think a great darkness will follow the present light, and after that the judgment day will come."

Distinction Between the Law and the Gospel

Winter of 1542–1543

"For a long time, I went astray [in the monastery] and didn't know what I was about. To be sure, I knew something, but I didn't know what it was until I came to the text in Romans 1 [:17], 'The one who is righteous will live by faith.' That text helped me. There I saw what righteousness Paul was talking about. Earlier in the text I read 'righteousness.' I related the abstract ['righteousness'] with the concrete ['the righteous One'] and became sure of my cause. I learned to distinguish between the righteousness of the law and the righteous-

---

33. Up to the fourth century the Epistle of James was not included in the canon by many Christian leaders, and earlier writers did not quote from it.

ness of the gospel. I lacked nothing before this except that I made no distinction between the law and the gospel. I regarded both as the same thing and held that there was no difference between Christ and Moses except the times in which they lived and their degrees of perfection. But when I discovered the proper distinction—namely, that the law is one thing and the gospel is another—I made myself free."

Then Dr. Pomeranus said, "I began to experience a change when I read about the love of God and what it signifies passively, namely, that by which we are loved by God. Before I had always taken love actively [namely, that by which we love God]."

The doctor [Martin Luther] said, "Yes, it is clear—by charity or by love!—that it's often understood [in the Scriptures] of that by which God loves us. However, in Hebrew the genitives of love' are difficult."

Then Pomeranus added, "Nevertheless, other passages afterward make these clear."

The Book of Proverbs Is Good for Rulers

Winter of 1542–1543

"Proverbs is an excellent book. Rulers ought to read it. There one can see how things happen in the world. There's nothing in the book but 'Fear God' and 'Pray.' On the other hand, we proceed with mathematics and counting and say that something amounts to so and so much. In this way, we propose to force our Lord God. Then he says, 'Ah, dear fellow, don't force me. No! No! . . .' 'The blessing of the Lord makes rich' [Prov 10:22]. It's so, too, with mining. That's the blessing of the Lord. They try to force our Lord God and his grace, but he won't let himself be forced. And then we lose everything. When we undertake something, no matter how small it may be, we should call upon our Lord God and pray and pray, even if he gives us only a piece of bread and a healthy body. Yet, we wish to blindfold him; we don't want him to see anything because we want to do it ourselves. This is what we do and experience to our great loss. This is what happens to princes and lords. They can't say with David, 'The one who gives victory to kings and who subdues the peoples under me' [Ps 144:10, 2]."

Promise for the Jews, Mercy for the Gentiles

Winter of 1542–1543

When the gospel was read at table by his son Martin,[34] "I was sent only to the lost sheep of the house of Israel" [Matt 15:24], the doctor [Martin Luther] said, "Christ seems to contradict himself because in this gospel he said, 'I was sent only to the lost sheep,' etc., and yet he saved the daughter of the [Canaanite] woman."

Master Holstein asked how this contradiction might be resolved. Thereupon he [Martin Luther] replied, "He wasn't sent to the heathen, but if they came to him he didn't reject them."

Then somebody else said, "Then he did not come for our sake?"

The doctor responded, "Christ was a servant to the circumcised to show God's truthfulness, as Paul wrote [Rom 15:8]. But when he came he found many Samaritans and Sadducees, as there are many epicureans[35] today, but he was supposed to preach in that land, and afterward he preached to the whole world through the apostles. Paul said that the Word of God should be spoken 'first to you. Since you reject it and judge yourselves to be unworthy of eternal life, we are now turning to the Gentiles' [Acts 13:46]. Christ was therefore sent to the Jews in person because they had the promise of his person. The Gentiles didn't have the promise but they had mercy [Rom 15:9]. He didn't speak to us but about us. He wished to test the woman's faith, and when she said, 'Lord, it's true, I don't deserve it, and I know that I didn't have the promise,' he heard her prayer."

---

34. Martin was eleven years old at this time.
35. I.e., skeptics.

4

Table Talks on the Sacraments

Rejection of Transubstantiation

November 9, 1531

"In the sacrament of the altar Thomas[1] invented transubstantiation. I think that the bread and wine remain, just as the water remains in baptism and just as the human voice remains when I preach. Yet it is in truth the power of God, as Paul calls it."[2]

Original Sin Is Like a Wound

Between November 30 and December 14, 1531

"After baptism, original sin is like a wound which has begun to heal. It is really a wound, yet it is becoming better and is constantly in the process of healing, although it is still festering, is painful, etc. So, original sin remains in the baptized until their death, although it is in the process of being rooted out. It is rendered harmless, and so it cannot accuse or damn us."

---

1. Thomas Aquinas (d. 1274), greatest of the medieval scholastic theologians.
2. Cf. Rom 1:16.

Left-wing and Right-wing Positions

Summer or Fall, 1532

"In their teaching about the sacraments, the papists go too far to the left, for they ascribe too much to the sacraments and claim that they justify by their mere observance. On the other hand, the sacramentarians[3] go too far to the right because they take everything away from the sacraments. Whether one falls out of the ship in front or behind, therefore, one lands in the water."

Administration of the Lord's Supper to Convicts

Summer or Fall, 1532

When a certain Bohemian said that the sacrament ought not to be given to those who have been convicted of a public crime and have been condemned in a public trial because there is danger that they might not believe, Luther responded, "This doesn't concern the one who administers. His only concern should be that he offer the true Word and the true sacrament. I don't worry about whether he [the communicant] has true faith. I give the sacrament on account of the confession which I have heard, the condition of his heart be what it may. I wager a thousand souls that the absolution and the sacrament are right. I must believe him when he says he is penitent. If he deceives me, he deceives himself. Nevertheless, the sacrament is true and the absolution is true. It is as if I were to give somebody ten pieces of gold and he took them to be only ten coppers. The gold is right in front of his eyes. If he doesn't know what he's taking, the fault is his and the loss is his."

Christ and Faith Must Be the Center

Summer or Fall, 1532

"Under the papacy, I was exposed to every error. The reason is that I had no faith. Faith is, as it were, the center of a circle. If any-

---

3. Luther's favorite term for those (especially Anabaptists and Zwinglians) who denied that the sacraments are means of grace. Luther put on the right those who are today generally placed on the left.

body strays from the center, it is impossible for him to have the circle around him, and he must blunder. The center is Christ."

No Compulsion to Observe Ceremonies

Summer or Fall, 1532

When somebody asked Martin Luther whether the sacrament [of the altar] ought to be adored, he replied, "One should not make an act of worship out of the sacrament. To be sure, I kneel, but I do so out of reverence. When I am lying in bed I receive it [the sacrament] without kneeling. It is a matter of freedom, just as one is at liberty to kiss the Bible or not. This might also be called adoration. If I do not do it, I have not sinned. But if anybody tries to compel me to do it as a thing necessary for salvation, I refuse and preserve my freedom."

The Word of God and the Sacraments

Fall, 1532

"The text, '[Let the little children come to me . . . for] it is to such as these that the kingdom of God belongs' [Mark 10:14], is the promise to Abraham. This text clearly speaks about children. One can't get around it. The text doesn't speak of adults, such as the apostles now were. Moreover, it says of children, 'to such belongs.' That is, 'I'm their Christ; I've been promised to them. I've also been promised to you adult Jews, but you've become too clever.' Thus, we have a promise and command for the baptism of children, because Christ said, 'Preach to all nations,'[4] as if he would say, 'I wish to be the God of all.' Circumcision was only for Abraham and the Jews, but baptism is for all nations, large and small, young and old. Circumcision doesn't save, but it was attached to the future Christ. Even so, the promise which is added makes baptism. Abraham had the Word along with circumcision. Hence baptism is no more than water, but the water has been surrounded by the Word. Baptism offers as much as circumcision used to. It was proper for Abraham to say, 'I have been circumcised, and in that circumcision Christ was promised to

---

4. Cf. Matt 28:19, 20.

me.' The promise does it. In the New Testament the promise is, 'I shall be your God,' and it is on this promise that you should be baptized. In itself circumcision was nothing. So, it doesn't help the Turks when they are circumcised[5] because the promise is lost. If the promise were absent I would thumb my nose at the water. Accordingly, the patriarchs received the promise, 'I will be your God;' and then they were circumcised. However, there is this difference between circumcision and baptism, namely, that circumcision was performed before Christ in anticipation of the very grace which is in baptism, while baptism is observed after Christ on the strength of the grace which he has secured. The grace is the same, and the only difference is between the past and future tense. However, both look to the last judgment when all will be revealed.

"The text about children ought not to be passed over lightly, but one ought to do what they say at court: The letter of a prince should be read three times. What does 'I am your God' mean except that he wishes to save us? Therefore, be circumcised as a sign. But the text, 'To such belongs the kingdom of heaven,' means to say, 'You adults are sons of the devil and have lost your childlikeness.' So, although certain persons have been baptized, when they grow up and don't believe they are nevertheless damned. The devil snatches them from their childlikeness.

"Children under the law accepted circumcision on account of that word, 'I am your God.' They didn't assent to it, yet those so circumcised were the people of God. Even so, a prince protects infants whom he hasn't known and who haven't known him. All this is accomplished by the covenant, the promised seed. Circumcision is no longer in full force now because it was intended to be performed only to the time of Christ. Signs have often been changed. In the time from Adam to Abraham people had only the sign of sacrifice, the burning of victims by fire.[6] That was a more magnificent sign than we have. Afterward Noah had a rainbow[7] and Abraham had circumcision.[8] I think that from that first sign of fire came the custom

---

5. Circumcision was practiced in Islam.
6. Cf. Gen 4:4.
7. Cf. Gen 4:4.
8. Cf. Gen 17:23.

of the Chaldeans to worship fire. Circumcision lasted from Abraham to the time of Christ, and after the time of Christ baptism has been used. Thus, the signs have become less and less, but the things and the deeds have grown increasingly.

"The sign and the promise should be tied to each other, not torn from each other. Those err who abandon the sign and say, 'God is the God of all nations and therefore I won't allow myself to be baptized.' For the promise always stands in such a way that the letter and the seal should be together. Neither avails without the other. One doesn't have faith in a seal which stands by itself, nor in a letter by itself. It is even so here. To be sure, it may be that if a person dies who was just baptized and stands upon the promise, he will be saved, but this is another question. Yet this remains firm, that signs are not to be neglected. And this is the reason we don't damn infants who die before they are baptized: the parents wish and intend to have them baptized. Consequently, don't judge such an infant but commend him to God. After baptism one should seek to do the same thing, for the Word and the sign are joined together. If you have the letter, let a seal be affixed to it. It would have availed nothing if a Jew had said, 'I am Abraham's son and therefore I don't want to be circumcised.'

"Because the objection is now raised that the day of circumcision was fixed—namely, the eighth day—but the time of baptism was not fixed, I reply: I'm not concerned about the work but about the Word. The eighth day adds nothing. Nor does either the command or the sign add anything, for Abraham was righteous before the circumcision. Learn to hold the Word high. It's true that circumcision was a command, a requirement, and was prescribed for the eighth day, but you should say, 'This day or that day, this command or that command—these aren't the important things. This is of central importance: that God is your God and the God of your seed. It's on the strength of this promise that you should be circumcised.' Even so, it doesn't matter whether one is baptized when young or old, but it matters that God is the God of young and old and that he gave his Son for them. It's on this that you should be baptized.

"No heathen could say, 'God is my God,' unless he heard the Word. Therefore, these statements are different: God is the Lord of all nations, and God is the God of all nations. For he's not the God of those who don't have his Word, just as he's not the God of the Jews who don't have his Word, even if they are circumcised. To be sure, he reveals himself to them, but they do not all accept him.

"As for the children, I think that all children who are baptized may be saved. With respect to predestination one should get so far as to say: If he doesn't have the Word, I commit him to God's judgment as to whether he gets it or not. If he doesn't he is lost. As far as we are concerned, we now have God's Word, and so we ought not have any doubt about our salvation. It's in this way that we should dispute about predestination, for it has already been settled: I have been baptized and I have the Word, and so I have no doubt about my salvation as long as I continue to cling to the Word. When we take our eyes off Christ we come upon predestination and start to dispute. Our Lord God says, 'Why don't you believe me? Yet you hear me when I say that you are beloved by me and your sins are forgiven.' This is our nature, that we are always running away from the Word.

"The papists have alarmed us with wicked thoughts about children who die. Here we must be careful. . . . Often mothers and midwives abandon infants who are born unexpectedly and might become horrible monstrosities. It does no harm, therefore, to keep these women in fear, lest they thoughtlessly let the children die. There are enough accidents without these. Consequently, we say and we warn that children be brought promptly for baptism." [Somebody asked] whether the Lord's Supper should be given to children. "I reply: There is no urgency about the sacrament of the altar. So, there's no command concerning prayer, but there's a precept that when we pray we should expect to be heard.[9] Nor is there a precept about afflictions, although those who are afflicted ought to be patient.[10] However, it doesn't follow that the children are damned who either do not pray or are not afflicted. When in 1 Corinthians [11:28] Paul said that a man should examine himself, he spoke only of adults because he was speaking about those who were quarreling among themselves. How-

---

9. Cf. 1 John 5:14.
10. Cf. 2 Cor 6:4.

ever, he doesn't here forbid that the sacrament of the altar be given even to children."

Christ in Sacrament Because He Is Ubiquitous

Spring, 1533

"Christ is truly in our hearts. People don't understand that God can do more than create heaven and earth and all things. So, I say, when you hear that God said so, you should ask, 'What's this, if God can do even more?' If he could make the world he could have created more worlds. Why, then, don't I believe that it is God's Word that says, 'This is my body' [1 Cor 11:24]?

"They reply, 'I don't believe because heaven and earth are so constituted that they require space.'

"To this I respond, 'Our Lord God made a world for men and another world for spirits. What if he had added a third world? He could have.' Why, then, do they argue against us?

"According to his divinity Christ is everywhere.... When I think of God I think of everything as a poppy seed in his eyes, and it is present wherever I am. Christ is God and man in one person. Where I seek God, there I find him. Accordingly, when we think of divinity we must turn our eyes away from time and space because our Lord God and Creator must be beyond space and time and creature."

Children Should Be Baptized on God's Command

Summer or Fall, 1533

"You say you don't baptize children because they don't believe. Why do you preach the Word to adults who don't believe, unless perhaps in the hope that they may believe? You do it on the strength of God's command alone. For if you baptize me because I say I believe, then you baptize on account of me and in my name. Therefore, since you don't know whether I believe or don't believe, you do it only because of God's command. It isn't necessary to exclude children, since as a rule you baptize all, whether they believe or not.

"It would be a terrible thing if I were baptized on the strength of my confession. What would you do if you learned privately that a man who publicly desired baptism or the sacrament [of the altar] was an unbeliever? You couldn't deny it to him, and yet you would know that he is without faith. So, Christ offered [the sacrament] to Judas.[11] Therefore, anybody at all should be baptized unless he has been publicly convicted of a crime, and let his faith and salvation be committed to God's keeping."

Meaning of Words Used in the Lord's Supper

Fall, 1533

"The question is asked, with reference to the words in the Lord's Supper, whether 'is given'[12] is to be understood as a present giving, when the sacrament is distributed, or as a [past] giving on the cross. I answer: I prefer that it be taken as a present giving. However, it can also be taken as a giving on the cross. This isn't prevented by the fact that Christ spoke in the present tense, 'which is given for you,' when he ought to have said, 'which will be given,' for Christ is the same yesterday and today [Heb 13:8]. 'I am the one who does it,' he says, 'and nobody else.' Accordingly, I prefer that 'is given' be understood as signifying the use of what has been done [on the cross]."

A Defense of the Baptism of Infants

Fall, 1533

"The church has baptized infants for a thousand years, and God has given the Holy Spirit to those who have been baptized as infants. Moreover, this conclusion is valid *a posteriori*, for Peter also infers this in Acts 10 [:44–47], 'We have preached Christ among the Gentiles, and God gave his testimony by the Holy Spirit,' etc. This is an argument from the act, or *a posteriori*. God gave his blessing to the Gentiles without the law, and therefore they are without the law.

"Second, for more than a thousand years the church has baptized infants. Moreover, because the church never existed except among

---

11. It was often speculated, for want of contrary evidence in the New Testament, that Judas participated in the Last Supper.
12. Cf. 1 Cor 11:23.

the baptized, and it was necessary that the church always exist, therefore infant baptism is true baptism. So, I argue *a priori* that Christ commanded that all nations be taught and baptized,[13] and this included children. Again, it isn't the minister as a person who baptizes, but it's Christ who baptizes. Now, if an infant is baptized by Christ, how can I take this away and say that he isn't baptized?

"The pope unwittingly kept baptism and the [sacrament of the] altar, and through the pope's priests, as through men who were drowsy and drunk, God gave the sacraments. The Anabaptists[14] and Waldensians[15] rest the sacraments on the faith of the person, and therefore they reject the baptism of infants, arguing that one ought first to teach and only afterward to baptize.[16] I respond: There Christ spoke not of the institution but of the effect [of baptism]. If I should hold that the baptism of children is without effect, it doesn't follow that they should be rebaptized when they grow up and believe, for if some at Mount [Sinai] hadn't believed in the law[17] (whether or not they believed in God), would it have been necessary to make a law again after they had come to believe? It's one thing to have the effect of a work and it's another to have the work. Everything depends on distinguishing between the work of God and the work of men. The work of God is unchangeable."

Ordination and the Administration of Sacraments

Early in the year 1535

"1. Men are not ordained in order to make or produce anything but to administer what they find in the church, for they do not produce or make baptism or the Word but are to give and administer these.

"2. Baptism is water and the Word. How? Does the minister make it so? No, but because it's Christ's institution. Bread and wine also become the body of Christ because Christ so ordained.

---

13. Cf. Matt 28:19.
14. Luther often used this term loosely, but here he had in mind those who practiced rebaptism.
15. Religious dissenters in late medieval France and Italy, the Waldensians established connections with the Protestant Reformers in the sixteenth century. They practiced infant baptism, in spite of Luther's lumping them together with Anabaptists.
16. Cf. Mark 16:16.
17. Cf. Exod 19:17—20:17.

"3. They [papal priests] haughtily arrogate to themselves the power to consecrate [and make the sacrament], a power which neither saints, nor angels, nor Mary had and which the entire assembly of laymen does not boast of having had in primitive times.

"4. Rather, where the Word (which is the most important thing) is, there is the kingdom of God. Consequently, all things are there: church, Christ, sacraments, ordination. So, Christ said, 'Go and teach all nations to observe all I have commanded you [Matt 28:19, 20], namely, you who are to be ordained. Through the doctors, he ordered the nations to observe his commandments. Moreover, he commanded them to take and eat [Matt 26:26]. So, Paul delivered this to the Corinthians and ordered suitable men to teach what had been delivered to them.[18] Note carefully that where it's conceded that the church and the Word exist, there it's conceded that the whole Christ exists and not merely some partial thing or part of Christ.

"The church can be excused thus [with respect to administering the Lord's Supper in one kind]: Just as a person who desires baptism, but dies beforehand, is baptized in his faith at the time of death instead of with water, although we would otherwise baptize all unto death, so those who desire both kinds but can't get them are like persons unknowingly held in captivity who nevertheless are communicated in both kinds by faith. God could also preserve his own in other ways, unknown to us, as long as there remains in them the knowledge and certain faith that it is according to Christ's institution that his true body and blood are in the sacrament. Then they are communicated in this faith, and no sin can harm them unto damnation because they were deceived and uninformed, doing what they did unknowingly. Accordingly, they are not damned if by chance the priest shows only the bread, for faith in Christ's institution swallows up everything. That people have kept this faith is evident from that hymn, 'With his flesh and his blood,' etc. At the same time this hymn shows that both kinds were once in use among the laity. I'll leave it at that, lest they [the papists] prohibit this hymn, though it comes from their church and was not composed by Luther."

---

18. Cf. 1 Cor 1:1, 23–26.

TABLE TALKS ON THE SACRAMENTS

No Concession on the Sacrifice of the Mass

Between January 8 and March 23, 1532

"At the diet [of Augsburg] the papists tried to frighten and threaten us. They wished us to agree that the mass is a sacrifice of praise merely to provide themselves with a subterfuge in the term 'sacrifice.' I'm ready to concede to them that the mass is a sacrifice of praise, provided they on their part concede that it's not only the priest at the altar but every communicant who 'sacrifices.'"

An Argument for the Baptism of Infants

Between June 18 and July 28, 1537

Luther spoke about the baptism of infants and said that there was a time when many postponed baptism in the case of infants because they thought, when they observed that children of Christian parents degenerated from religion to an evil life, that it was safer to defer baptism until adolescence, lest it be contaminated and in order that it might rather be honored when received by those who were more mature. What appeared to be mistaken piety became the occasion for something bad, for St. Augustine and many others proceeded from postponement of baptism to such contempt of it that they were unwilling to be baptized.

Luther then related a story from Augustine's *Confessions*[19] according to which a certain unbaptized companion of Augustine was baptized by his parents when he was in the agony of death. When Augustine, who was then still a youth, visited him and scoffed at the baptism, the companion responded, "Be still, my dear Augustine, and do not attack holy baptism, God's covenant, in this way. I have been baptized, and on this I will die." With these words, he discouraged Augustine from his frivolous objection. It is therefore safer to baptize infants.

Then he [Luther] proposed a syllogism concerning the baptism of infants: "Either there has been no church or baptism had no effect.

---

19. Augustine, *Confessions*, IV, 4.

But it is impossible that there has been no church for fourteen hundred years. Therefore, the baptism of infants has been effective."

Hungarians Not to Have Separate Communion

September 22, 1538

On that day, certain Hungarian students asked for the sacrament in both kinds.[20] But since they did not understand the German language they requested that the sacrament be administered to them privately in Latin. Luther replied that the wish to communicate privately would give a bad example in the church. Even if they do not understand the words, nevertheless they know that this is the true ordinance of God and institution of Christ, Christ's testament, and that in our church it is offered publicly and in common through the Word and in the Word. Therefore, they ought never separate themselves from the church, for it would be much safer for their consciences and less offensive to the church if they would take the sacrament in the public fellowship And this is what they did, obediently and thankfully.

The Roman Mass as a Sacrifice to God

December 5, 1538

On December 5, there was much talk about the pestilential error concerning man's own righteousness, which has drawn even the best of men away from the truth of God. "The Jews made their sacrifices *ex opere operato*[21] in order that they might be expiation and satisfaction [for sin], as if they tossed a scrap to angry Cerberus[22] (though the only scrap is Christ), when all their sacrifices ought ultimately to be those of thanks and benevolence. Similar is the error of the papists concerning the sacrifice of the mass *ex opere operato,* when the priest, who is a stupid dolt and knows no Latin, atones for the sins of all men."

Then Luther began to say many things about the profanation of

---

20. I.e., in evangelical fashion, with distribution of wine as well as bread to the communicants.
21. A technical term in the late Middle Ages meaning by the mere performance of the act.
22. A three-headed dog in Greek mythology who guarded the entrance to the lower world.

the mass, which has held captive all men, both those who say mass and those who are bystanders. "The severest punishment for a masspriest [he said] was to forbid him to hold masses, for to celebrate mass was to do everything. It's not at all surprising therefore if the mass isn't abrogated very soon in England, for it puts on a great show."

Apart from Its Use a Sacrament Is Nothing

June 3, 1539

Then he [Martin Luther] was asked whether the sacraments have a spiritual power in themselves, so that baptism would be consecrated water which by its own strength could wipe out sins, even in case the water were drunk by an ass. He replied, "Because the spiritual power of God doesn't consist of corporeal, inanimate matter, baptism doesn't accomplish anything at all as water existing by itself. But as an action (which would be in its use) baptism has power, so that if anybody sprinkles an infant with water together with a recitation of those words of Christ by which he instituted baptism and promised the forgiveness of sins, that action, and not the water, has divine power. Thus, the sacraments are nothing apart from the action and use...."

Should a Liar Be Given the Sacrament?

Between September 18 and 23, 1540

"Doctor, if there is a scarcity of crops, and I admonish a rich man in confession that he should give something for the use of the poor and he denies that he has anything left over, but I know that he has, should I give the sacrament to such a liar?"

The doctor [Martin Luther] replied, "If he should deny it, what more can you do? If he persists, do what Christ did; he gave the sacrament to the betrayer Judas...."[23]

---

23. Cf. John 13:25-26.

Does the Kind of Water Affect Valid Baptism?

Summer or Fall, 1542

The doctor [Martin Luther]: "I wish to ask Dr. Jacob whether children should be baptized in warm water."

Dr. Jacob: "Yes."

Dr. Luther: "This becomes a change of elements,[24] and cold water terrifies like the law."

Dr. Jacob: "The cold is accidental. Besides, the law is often called fire too."

Dr. Luther: "It's true. Water that's too hot can also terrify, if this is to be determinative."

Dr. Jacob: "Should a child be baptized with wine? I hear that such a thing happened," etc.[25]

Dr. Luther: "If it's done, it's done by accident. So, in this instance what happened was that in an emergency the poor women laid hold of wine, thinking it was something else. That child shouldn't be baptized again because when I take something to be something—when I think it's water, even if it really is something else—there's no danger at all. Under the papacy priests often elevated water instead of wine."[26]

A Substitute for Wine in the Sacrament?

Winter of 1542–1543

When somebody inquired whether, when a sick person wished to have the sacrament but could not tolerate wine on account of nausea, something else should be given in place of the wine, the doctor [Martin Luther] replied, "This question has often been put to me and I have always given this answer: One shouldn't use anything else than wine. If a person can't tolerate wine, omit it [the sacrament] altogether in order that no innovation may be made or introduced. Is it

---

24. It used to be debated whether when heat was added to water the water was changed to another element.
25. There is a report of such a case when the child of Dr. Melchior Kling was baptized where it also appears that an emergency baptism was administered, presumably by midwives.
26. Priests, especially if nearsighted, easily mistook the cruet of water for the cruet of white wine at the altar. To prevent such confusion the use of red wine was recommended.

necessary for a person who is dying to have the sacrament again at the last moment?

"Formerly it was said that he who has consumed one kind should think that he has consumed both.[27] Why shouldn't we say, 'If you have taken neither, think that you have taken both'?"

On Administering the Sacrament to Oneself

Spring, 1543

The doctor [Martin Luther] was asked whether a man who was about to die and couldn't have the whole sacrament[28] from the papists did the right thing when he administered the sacrament to himself. He replied, "No! At least two persons must always be there, the one who gives and the one who receives. So, in an emergency a woman can baptize, but the child doesn't baptize himself. If a person can't have access to the sacrament, faith is enough, according to that word, 'Your faith has made you well' [Matt 9:22]. On the other hand, if he can have it, he should not despise it.

"Ambrose said something similar in a certain passage. He had a catechumen whom he converted to the faith. When he was on a journey to go to Ambrose in order to be baptized by him, the catechumen died on the way. This gave Ambrose troubled thoughts and he said, 'I have a pain in my stomach.' He misused the words in the prophet [Jer 4:19]. By these words, he meant to signify that he deplored that the catechumen should be lost to the people. At length, after long disputation, he also concluded that the catechumen was saved by his faith without baptism inasmuch as he thought properly of baptism and didn't despise it and would have had himself baptized in this faith if he had been able to. I have had many questions like this. . . . But it isn't right for a person to administer the sacrament to himself."

---

27. That is, the medieval church had taught that when laymen received only bread (the body of Christ) in the sacrament of the altar they really received the wine (the blood of Christ) as well, according to the theory of sacramental concomitance. Luther's argument here is ironical.

28. I.e., the wine as well as the bread in the Lord's Supper.

The Necessity of the Sacrament

Spring, 1543

When he was asked whether it was enough for a person to confess his sins and believe in absolution and not use the sacrament [of the altar], he [Martin Luther] replied, "No! It is stated in the words of institution, 'Do this in remembrance of me' [1 Cor 11:25]. Everything that is required of a Christian must be in the sacrament: acknowledgment of sin (which we call contrition), faith, giving of thanks, confession. These things must not be separated from one another."

Can the Minister Affect the Sacrament?

1544

[The question was asked] whether it would be permissible to receive the sacrament from a minister who himself thinks and teaches that the body and blood [of Christ] are not in the sacrament, but Christ is present spiritually, as he is present everywhere in his grace. Some say Yes on the ground that there should be no respect of persons or of the worthiness of those who administer the sacrament. Dr. Martin [Luther] said No on the ground that in this instance it is not the worthiness of the person but the thing itself that would cease.

"There's no sacrament there," he said. "Likewise, if the minister doesn't observe the sacrament in the right way, the people dare not act contrary to the Christ who shed his blood for them. O Lord God, anybody who can't believe that Christ is in the bread, in the grain of wheat, will believe the creation even less! That all of creation was made from nothing is a higher article of faith. Much less will he believe that God became man, and least of all that there are three persons in one substance. Reason lets this alone. It's an easy thing for me to believe that the body of Christ is in the bread, but it's hard to believe that so many excellent bodies in heaven and on earth should have come from nothing. I can't comprehend this. It's impossible for me. Much less can I comprehend that the Son was born of the Virgin Mary and that the other two persons [of the Trinity] did not become incarnate. If people are offended by this article, if they don't learn the ABC's, how will they learn their Donatus?[29] The article of creation is a lofty thing which no man can comprehend. So, the Holy Scriptures remain hidden to the clever and the wise, as St. Paul said [1 Cor 1:18–2:13]. If they don't believe this, the consequence will quickly follow. The Word of God—no, God himself—is seated at the right hand of the Father, and yet I am here in the living Word of God. 'In him we live and move and have our being' [Acts 17:28]. Where, then, will my life remain?"

---

29. The Latin grammar by Aelius Donatus, who lived in the fourth century, was so widely used at the close of the Middle Ages that his name had become synonymous with grammar.

5

Table Talks on Theology and Theologians

Value of Knowledge Gained by Experience

Summer or Fall, 1531

"A doctor of the Scriptures ought to have a good knowledge of the Scriptures and ought to have grasped how the prophets run into one another. It isn't enough to know only one part—as one might know Isaiah, for example—or to know only one topic of the law or of the gospel. Now, however, doctors are springing up who scarcely have a right comprehension of one topic.

"Teachers of law can humble their students when the students try to put on airs about their learning, because they have a court and get practical experience. On the other hand, we can't humble our students because we have no practical exercises. Yet experience alone makes the theologian."

About Augustine and Justification

Early November, 1531

"It was Augustine's[1] view that the law, fulfilled by the powers of reason, does not justify, even as works of the moral law do not justify the heathen, but that if the Holy Spirit assists, the works of the law do justify. The question is not whether the law or the works of reason justify, but whether the law, kept with the Spirit's help, justifies.

"I reply by saying No. Even if, in the power of the Holy Spirit, a man were to keep the law completely, he ought nevertheless to pray for divine mercy, for God has ordained that man should be saved not by the law but by Christ. Works never give us a peaceful heart. Christ would never have been sad in spirit unless he had been pressed hard by the law, to which he subjected himself for our sake."

Practical Versus Speculative Theology

Between December 14, 1531, and January 22, 1532

"True theology is practical, and its foundation is Christ, whose death is appropriated to us through faith. However today all those who do not agree with us and do not share our teaching make theology speculative because they cannot free themselves from the notion that those who do good [will be rewarded]. This is not what is written, but rather, 'Those who fear the Lord will have a happy end' [Ecclus 1:13]. Accordingly, speculative theology belongs to the devil in hell. So, Zwingli speculated, 'The body of Christ is in the bread, but only spiritually because I think it is in the bread.' Such is the theology of Origen also. David did not do it thus but acknowledged his sin and said, 'Have mercy on me, O God' [Ps 51:1]."

Nature Is Not Abolished by Grace

Between January and March, 1532

"Grace does not entirely change nature but uses nature as it finds it. So, if somebody is kind when converted through faith, he becomes a gentle preacher like Master Hausmann. If he is by nature irascible and severe, like Cordatus, he preaches after this fashion. On the other hand, if he is fitted by nature with some slyness, intelligence, and power of reason, like Philip, he uses these qualities for the benefit of mankind."

---

1. Luther probably was thinking of Augustine's *Against Two Epistles of the Pelagians*, 3, 20.

The Omnipresence of God

Between April 7 and 15, 1532

When we were debating whether God truly is in each and every minute creature, in the grass, in a tree, etc., he [Martin Luther] responded, "It is so, for God is excluded from no place and is confined to none. He is everywhere and he is nowhere."

The question was asked whether God is only potentially everywhere or is actually everywhere. He replied, "God is in every creature in both ways because although a creature acts through its properties, God acts not through his properties but through his being."

Thereupon somebody said, "I do not understand that."

He [Luther] countered, "Do you believe that Christ on the cross was God?"

"Yes."

"Do you believe that God was in the womb of the Virgin?"

"Yes."

"The principle here is the same, for it is equally impossible to man's reason in both cases, as impossible that God can be enclosed in the womb of the Virgin as it is that he can be enclosed in every creature."

Thereupon the other person said, "Then he is in the devil too!"

"Yes, and essentially! He's in hell too, as it is written in 2 Thessalonians 1 [:9], 'These will suffer the punishment of eternal destruction, separated from the presence of the Lord.'"

God Is Unknowable and Yet Known

Between April 20 and May 16, 1532

"In his dialogue concerning being, Plato[2] disputes about God and declares that God is nothing and yet is everything. Eck followed Plato, and other theologians also said that the affirmative definition is uncertain but the negative definition is absolute. Nobody has understood this. It ought to be put and can be understood thus: 'God is incomprehensible and invisible, and hence whatever is comprehended and seen is not God.' It can also be expressed in another way:

---

2. Intended is probably Plato's *Timaeus*, 27.

'God is both visible and invisible. He is visible through his Word and work. Apart from his Word and work one should not look for him.' These theologians have wished to apprehend God through speculations and have paid no attention to the Word. I recommend that speculation be laid aside, and I should like to have this rule adhered to after my death."

Theology Is Not Quickly Learned

Fall, 1532

"Clever men see that the church is despised and that others are exalted. They judge according to reason, without the Word of God, and thus reach this conclusion. Hence it comes to pass that they despise all religion and say that the article concerning the resurrection was only invented to terrify the common people. Peasants, however, seldom go so far as to despise God and religion, for they hardly think about such things. But clever people are interested in them, reflect upon them, and weigh them according to reason. . . . But we know that the Holy Scriptures are confirmed, as no other teaching can be, by such miracles as the raising of the dead, the expulsion of demons, etc. It is for this reason that our Lord God warns us so often to abide by the Holy Scriptures.

"I didn't learn my theology all at once. I had to ponder over it ever more deeply, and my spiritual trials were of help to me in this, for one does not learn anything without practice. This is what the spiritualists and sects lack. They don't have the right adversary, the devil. He would teach them well. None of the arts can be learned without practice. What kind of physician would that be who stayed in school all the time? When he finally puts his medicine to use and deals more and more with nature, he will come to see that he hasn't as yet mastered the art. Why shouldn't this be so in the case of the Holy Scriptures, too, where God has provided a different adversary? It is therefore the greatest gift [of God] to have a text and to be able to say, 'This is right. I know it.' People think that they can know everything by simply listening to a sermon. Zwingli also made the mistake of thinking that he knew everything, that theology is an easy art. But

I know that I have yet to comprehend the Lord's Prayer. No one can be learned without practice. The peasant put it well: Armor is fine for a man who knows how to use it. To be sure, the Holy Scriptures are sufficient in themselves, but God grant that I find the right text. For when Satan disputes with me whether God is gracious to me, I dare not quote the passage, 'He who loves God will inherit the kingdom of God,'[3] because Satan will at once object, 'But you have not loved God!' Nor can I oppose this on the ground that I am a diligent reader [of the Scriptures] and a preacher. The shoe doesn't fit.[4] I should say, rather, that Jesus Christ died for me and should cite the article [of the Creed] concerning forgiveness of sin. That will do it!"

Difference Between a Lawyer and a Theologian

December, 1532

"The lawyer says: Let justice be done and the world be damned.[5] The theologian says: Let sin be forgiven and the world will be saved, for justice is not done but sin is always committed."

The Kind of God Men Think They Have

December, 1532

"When an epicurean thinks about God and observes how things happen in the world, he can't do otherwise than conclude: Either God can't stop these things, and then he must be very weak; he must not be omnipotent. Or else he doesn't want to stop them, and then he must be very wicked, for he delights in evils. Or again, he doesn't know what is happening, and then he must be very foolish. So, God is unduly deprived of his power, his justice, and his wisdom. . . ."

---

3. Cf. 1 Cor 2:9.
4. Literally, the horseshoe is not attached properly. That is, this kind of argument does not meet the need.
5. Proverbial saying adopted by Emperor Ferdinand as his motto.

Forgiveness of Sin Is Hard to Believe

Early in the year 1533

"It's impossible for our adversaries to understand the forgiveness of sins because they are immersed in their notion of quality.[6] The Holy Scriptures call Christians saints and the people of God. It's a pity that it's forgotten that we are saints, for to forget this is to forget Christ and baptism. (In Psalm 86 [:2] the Hebrew for 'I am a saint,' *chasid,* means the opposite, 'I am cursed.') So, it comes about that those who are truly sinners don't want to be considered sinners, and those who are saints don't want to be called saints either. The latter don't believe the gospel which comforts them and the former don't believe the law which accuses them.

"You say that the sins which we commit every day offend God, and therefore we are not saints. To this I reply: Mother love is stronger than the filth and scabbiness on a child, and so the love of God toward us is stronger than the dirt that clings to us. Accordingly, although we are sinners, we do not lose our filial relation on account of our filthiness, nor do we fall from grace on account of our sin.

"You object that we are always sinning, and where there are sins the Holy Spirit does not dwell; therefore we are not saints because the Spirit sanctifies. I reply: The text says, 'The Spirit will glorify me' [John 16:13,14]. Therefore, where Christ is, there is the Holy Spirit also. Besides, sins do not separate Christ from sinners who believe. The God of the Turks helps only to the extent that one is godly. This is also true of the pope's God, but when a papist begins to doubt, as he must, that he has made enough satisfaction, he becomes alarmed. Such is the faith of the pope and the Turks. But the Christian says: I believe and cling to him who is in heaven as a Savior. If I fall into sin I rise again but don't continue to sin. I rise up and become the enemy of sin. Thus, the Christian faith differs from other religions in this, that the Christian hopes even in the midst of evils and sins. Without the Holy Spirit, human beings can't do this. They can only seek refuge in works. To say, 'I am a child of God,' is accordingly not to doubt even when good works are lacking, as they always are in all of

---

6. Variant reads: 'their notion of the righteousness that remains in them.'

us. This is so great a thing that one is startled by it. Such is its magnitude that one can't believe it."

Signs of the End of the World

February, 1533

"The passage[7] about the calamities of the last days I don't understand to refer to physical punishment, for the text is sure: at its end the world will be very happy, powerful, proud, and secure.[8] You see this now. I hardly have a better sign of the last day than this. Besides, the Word is also held in the greatest contempt. All these things are now happening. Blessed is he who understands them! But hardly anybody perceives them."

Predestination Related to the Grace of God

Spring, 1533

"Concerning the statement, 'So it depends not on human will or exertion, but on God who shows mercy' [Rom 9:16], I respond: In this passage Paul was doing nothing less than disputing about predestination, but he was speaking against the Jews and the righteousness of the law and he meant to say, 'You must despair, give God the glory, and confess that you didn't start it.' When I was a monk I depended on such willing and exertion, but the longer [I worked at it] the farther away I got. What I have now I have not from exertion but from God. So, in this passage Paul was saying everything against presumption, so that we may say, 'Lord, whatever [good] there is in us exists by thy grace.'

"So, he also appeals to that saying, 'I will have mercy on whom I have mercy' [Rom 9:15], that is, 'you won't do it without my forgiveness.' In short, all this is spoken against those who are proud: 'He to whom I give it will have it; you are not to win it from me by your holiness.' What more should he do? He says, 'You are to have it. But when you seek it and insist on having it because of your righteous-

---

7. Cf. Matt 24:21.
8. Cf. Matt 24:37, 38.

ness, I won't suffer it. I would rather throw everything away—priesthood, kingdom, even my law. But expect grace from me, and you will have it.'"

When somebody inquired whether a person [under the papacy] would be saved if he had not embraced this teaching of ours, he [Martin Luther] replied, "I really don't know. God might have had regard for his baptism. This could do it. Even so, I have seen many [monks] die with a crucifix held before their eyes [as was then customary]. In spite of everything else, the name [of Christ] proved to be effective on their deathbed."

Predestination Is an Impenetrable Mystery

Spring, 1533

"Paul wasn't discussing predestination with the Jews but was disputing only with those who opposed it and said, 'We are the people of God, we have the fathers, the promises were given to us,' etc. He didn't touch upon predestination except[9] to repudiate the righteousness of the law. Paul said that we should not preach as if we could become good by our works, our fathers, etc. These don't help. The others, those who believe, have it just as good as those who have fathers, etc. God has decreed it so from eternity. Hence Paul attacks only this.

"By grace alone are we saved. God doesn't want to be obligated to anybody. Once we believe, he tells us (and this, too, is 'by grace), 'Give, and it will be given to you' [Luke 6:38]. You are bound to give in any case, whether out of pity for the Turks or some other unfortunates, so you may just as well do it when I command it.' We have no claim on him. So, Esau and Jacob also testified to righteousness.[10]

"Otherwise one can't settle the deep questions of theology, but Paul simply argues that it is by grace alone that we are saved. He meant to stick to this. Think what it means that you are not saved by the law, etc., but the Jews have works! Nobody but Christ can solve

---

9. Cf. Rom 9: 15.
10. Cf. Gen 24:1—35:29.

this. Hence, he [Paul] said, 'O the depth [of the riches and wisdom and knowledge of God,' Rom 11:33]!"

Luther Expresses His Thanks for Staupitz

Spring, 1533

"Our Lord God is our Lord. He calls us and therefore we must preach. Otherwise who would endure the hatred? For contempt and ingratitude have increased greatly. However, my good Staupitz said, 'One must keep one's eyes fixed on that man who is called Christ.' Staupitz is the one who started the teaching [of the gospel in our time]."

Heretics Provoke Theologian to Search Scriptures

Fall, 1533

"Anybody who wishes to be a theologian must have a fair mastery of the Scriptures, so that he may have an explanation for whatever can be alleged against any passage. That is to say, he must distinguish between law and gospel. If I were able to do this perfectly I would never again be sad. Whoever apprehends this has won.

"Whatever is Scripture is either law or gospel. One of the two must triumph: the law leads to despair; the gospel leads to salvation. I learn more about this every day. . . . The gospel is life. The pope drove me to this; he opened my eyes to it. It is as Augustine said to himself: the heretics provoke us to search the Scriptures. Otherwise nobody would think about them."

The Defects of Speculative or Mystical Theology

Fall, 1533

"The speculative learning of the theologians is altogether worthless. I have read Bonaventure[11] on this, and he almost drove me mad because I desired to experience the union of God with my soul (about

---

11. Bonaventure (1221–1274) was a Franciscan whose mystical and dialectical writings occupy an important place in the history of medieval thought.

which he babbles) through a union of intellect and will. Such theologians are nothing but fanatics. This is the true speculative theology (and it's practical too): Believe in Christ and do what you ought. Likewise, the mystical theology of Dionysius[12] is nothing but trumpery, and Plato prattles that everything is non-being and everything is being, and he leaves it at that. This is what mystical theology declares: Abandon your intellect and senses and rise up above being and non-being.

"Is being in such shadows? God is everything," etc.

We Trust Human Beings More Than We Trust Christ

Between January 8 and March 23, 1532

"The principal lesson of theology is that Christ can be known. Here the teacher shouldn't be ashamed of learning from his student, nor the student of learning from his teacher. Christ is friendlier than we are. If I can be good to a friend, how much more will Christ be good to us! When Satan leads me to the law I am damned, but if I can take hold of the promise I am free. Peter said, 'Grow in the knowledge of Christ' [2 Pet 3:18]. This isn't a knowledge of the law, of dialectical skill, or of some other art, but it's the knowledge that Christ is the most just and the most merciful One, in whom alone we dwell. Satan clouds this basic knowledge in our hearts in a remarkable way and causes us to trust an earthly friend more than Christ."

Lawyers and Theologians in Similar Position

Between January 8 and March 23, 1532

"Lawyers will have the same experience that we theologians have. Because we theologians tell the truth, people are hostile to us and persecute us. If you lawyers would also speak to the nobles about their virtues, their usury, etc., your lot would be the same as ours. Lawyers now tend to despise us, though they got from us whatever

---

12. Dionysius the Areopagite was converted to Christianity by St. Paul, and it became customary in the Middle Ages to ascribe to him a number of mystical writings which probably originated in the fifth or sixth century.

they know. In short, we say that the lawyers are incompetent, and so they say that we theologians are incompetent."

The Tempted and Afflicted Understand the Gospel

Between May 20 and 27, 1532

"There is only one article and one rule of theology, and this is true faith or trust in Christ. Whoever doesn't hold this article and this rule is no theologian. All other articles flow into and out of this one; without it the others are meaningless. The devil has tried from the very beginning to deride this article and to put his own wisdom in its place. However, this article has a good savor for all who are afflicted, downcast, troubled, and tempted, and these are the ones who understand the gospel."

Conversation After the Elector's Funeral

August 18, 1532

"It's hard to get away from thinking about works, for God wants them and commands them. But he doesn't want us to rely on them and record them. He says, 'I'll repay you well for them. Don't give the matter a thought and don't demand a reward for them. . . .'"

The Pope and the Ecclesiological Problem

Between February 9 and 12, 1533

"The issue in the controversy over the papacy is that the pope boasts that he's the head of the church and condemns all who don't live under his power, for he says that although Christ is the [spiritual] head of the church, there must nevertheless also be a bodily head on earth. (I would gladly have conceded this to the pope if he had only taught the gospel.) In addition, he claims for himself authority over the church and the Scriptures. No one may expound the Scriptures except the pope alone, who does it as he pleases. He boasts that he is lord over the church and the church in turn is mistress over the Scriptures, and so everybody must submit to him. This was intolerable to me and provoked me to write against the papacy. Our opponents still admit today that our teaching's true, but they defend themselves by saying that it's not yet approved by the pope.

"Duke George, our bitterest foe, admits the same thing. On the day of judgment, I intend to speak candidly to him like this: 'Listen, Duke George, do you believe that you are baptized? Do you believe that the Lord's Supper was instituted by Christ in both kinds? Do you believe that our doctrine is true?'

"Then he will reply, 'I believe, but because the pope hasn't approved,' etc.

"Begone to your own god, for you have been unwilling to give honor to God.

"Those who thus put their reliance on the church, contrary to the plain Word, are very silly. It's as if one were to say, 'I'd like to love the son, but I must first kill the mother.' They attribute more to the church that is created than to the Word that creates. But, thank God, we have the testimony that we are not heretics but only schismatics, and they are to blame for our separation."

Description of Luther's "Tower Experience"

Between June 9 and July 21, 1532

"The words 'righteous' and 'righteousness of God' struck my conscience like lightning. When I heard them, I was exceedingly terrified. If God is righteous[13] [I thought], he must punish. But when by God's grace I pondered, in the tower and heated room of this building, over the words, 'The one who is righteous will live by faith' [Rom 1:17] and 'the righteousness of God' [Rom 3:21], I soon came to the conclusion that if we, as righteous people, ought to live from faith and if the righteousness of God should contribute to the salvation of all who believe, then salvation won't be our merit but God's mercy. My spirit was thereby cheered. For it's by the righteousness of God that we're justified and saved through Christ. These words [which had before terrified me] now became more pleasing to me. The Holy Spirit unveiled the Scriptures for me in this tower."

---

13. The Latin word *ustus* can be translated either by 'righteous' or by 'just.'

The Church Not Built by Ceremonies

Spring, 1533

"The papists, the fanatics, and whoever they may be who set their own opinions against the gospel are already condemned with all their wisdom, holiness, and beliefs. For our wiseacres do nothing except to slander us and say, 'Luther has indeed destroyed the papacy but he can't build a new church,' that is, can't introduce a new form of worship and new ceremonies. These wretched men think that building up the church consists of the introduction of some sort of new ceremonies. They don't realize that building up the church means to lead consciences from doubt and murmuring to faith, to knowledge, and to certainty."

Difference Between the Two Kingdoms

Fall, 1533

"Our Lord God has reserved the best rule for himself and his church, where one proceeds not in the exercise of law but in voluntary freedom. For Christ says, 'I baptize you, I catechize you, I absolve you, I preach to you, I comfort you. If you believe, you have this treasure. If you don't believe, the loss is yours. I don't forfeit anything as a consequence.'

"On the other hand, civil rule proceeds by demand: 'Do this, don't do that!' 'If you don't obey,' says the magistrate, 'and you do me an injury, I'll punish you. However, if you obey me, it will be of benefit to me.'

"Thus, the civil government seeks its advantage with certain rigid demands. Christ's rule, however, looks to our benefit and allows us pleasing discretion. This works out well in the case of the elect. But in the case of civil rulers, the more they demand with their rigorous laws, 'Thus and so it must be done,' the less well it works out."

A Blast Against Agricola's Antinomianism

March 21, 1537

After this conversation, Master Jobst showed him [Martin Luther] statements which declared that the law should not be preached in the church because it does not justify. Deeply moved, he [Martin Luther] said, "To think that this should be said by our own people even in our lifetime! This is the opinion of Agricola, who is driven by hatred and ambition. Would that we might pay heed to Master Philip! Philip teaches clearly and eloquently about the function of the law. I am inferior to him although I have also treated this topic clearly in my Galatians.[14]

"The prophecy that was written to me by Count Albrecht is being fulfilled, namely, that there's something of a Münzer behind this.[15] For anybody who abolishes the teaching of the law in a political context abolishes government and domestic life, and anybody who abolishes the law in an ecclesiastical context ceases to have a knowledge of sin. The gospel doesn't expose sin except through the law, which is spiritual and which defines sin as opposition to God's will. Away with him who claims that transgressors don't sin against the law but only dishonor the Son of God! Such speculative theologians are the bane of the churches. Without a conscience, without knowledge, and without logical discrimination they teach everything confusedly and say things like this, 'Love is the fulfilment of the law,'[16] and therefore we have no need of the law.' But those wretched fellows neglect the minor premise: that this fulfilment (namely, love) is weak in our flesh, that we must struggle daily against the flesh with the help of the Spirit, and this belongs under the law."

Justification Explained by an Analogy

June 18, 1537
Martin Luther gave a very clear and apt explanation of the article of justification by showing its resemblance to the relation of a father and a son in this way: "A son is born an heir, is not made one, and inherits his father's goods without any work or merit. Meanwhile,

---

14. *Lectures* on *Galatians* (1535).
15. I.e., there is something fanatical about this, as there was in the teaching of Thomas Münzer, who advocated rebellion against the princes and became a leader in the Peasants' War, in which he lost his life.
16. Cf. Rom 13:10.

however, the father commands and exhorts his son to be diligent in doing this or that. He promises him a reward or a gift in order that in return for it he may obey more readily and freely: 'If you're good and listen, if you study diligently, I'll buy you a nice coat. Come here to me and I'll give you a beautiful apple.' In this way, the father helps his son in his weakness, although the inheritance belongs to him on other grounds. This is done for the sake of pedagogy.

"God also deals with us in this way. He coaxes us with promises of spiritual and physical things, although eternal life is given freely to those who believe in Christ as children of adoption, etc. So, it ought to be taught in the church that God will repay good works, save in the article of justification, which is the origin and source of all other promises. One should say, 'Believe and you will be saved; do what you will, it won't help you [to be saved].' Accordingly, we should remember that those promises and rewards are the pedagogy by which God, as a very gentle father, invites and entices us to do good, serve our neighbor," etc.

Proper and Improper Uses of Consecration

Between June 18 and July 28, 1537

Master Gabriel, pastor in Torgau, asked Dr. Martin Luther about that passage of Paul to Timothy [1 Tim 4:5], "For it is sanctified by God's word and by prayer."

Dr. Martin Luther replied, "Godly people acknowledge that all things are of God and consecrate them through the Word of God when they pray. To them all things are pure when they are used according to God's will. This passage doesn't support the papists who argue thus: Water that's been blessed has the Word of God; you despise holy water; therefore, you despise the Word of God.

"I answer: This isn't the will and command of God. Rather, it's an abomination to suppose that we cause water to be above nature and to become something beneficial to the soul. We don't say grace to make our food better than it had been before; if we think the food is health-bringing on this account it is an abuse of the Word of God. This abuse is accordingly to be carefully distinguished from a true use of the Word of God according to divine command. One shouldn't rely on the first word of God that comes along, for every abuse, error, and impiety has its origin in the Lord's name. Consecration is a pure and permitted practice, as in the letter to the Corinthians, 'The unbelieving husband is consecrated through his believing wife' [1 Cor 7:14], that is, sexual intercourse is in such a case pure and permitted."

Speculations About Predestination Unhealthy

December 25, 1537

He [Martin Luther] spoke at length about the idle people who occupy themselves with disputation about predestination beyond the limits of Scripture. "It is the most ungodly and dangerous business to abandon the certain and revealed will of God in order to search into the hidden mysteries of God."

Questions About Purgatory, Prayer, Free Will

January 10, 1538

On that day, a certain student came to him [Martin Luther] to ask his opinion about some doubts of his. He read aloud, from Eck's *Common Places,* the first section on purgatory, where Eck tried to prove his doctrine from the fathers. Luther replied that neither Ambrose nor Augustine nor Jerome had anything to say about purgatory, but Gregory, who was deceived by visions, taught something about purgatory, although God has forbidden that anything should be searched out with the help of spirits and has commanded that Moses and the prophets be heard. On this subject, therefore, no authority is to be attributed to St. Jerome. Eck and others interpret the passage in Paul's letter to the Corinthians, "for the Day [will disclose it, because it will be revealed with fire, and the fire will test what sort of work each has done," 1 Cor 3:13], as referring to purgatory, although this passage has nothing to say about purgatory but about doctrine and the good and the evil life of the godly and heretics. Arius[17] had his day and all heretics have had their day and judgment, but the fire of faith revealed it, as the last day will reveal all things.

In short, God has set before us two ways in his Word, the way to salvation through faith and the way to damnation through unbelief. There is no mention of purgatory. Nor should purgatory be admitted because it obscures the benefits and grace of Christ. However, it may be admitted to the sphere of the world [where true Christians are winnowed and purged].

Another question was raised about the intercession of saints, whether the dead pray for us. Luther replied, "Let's permit them to pray! Yet both their life and their prayer are unknown to us. We can't understand how their death is life. If it should be objected that St. Ambrose made an entreaty in behalf of Emperor Theodosius[18] after the latter's death, this was an invention of his. If it should be objected that Augustine prayed for his mother Monica [after her death], this proves nothing, nor did he wish his writings to be adhered to unless they agreed with the Holy Scriptures, for he wrote, 'I do not wish that my writings,' etc. In short, it's necessary to stick to the clear Word of God and not to human opinions."

There was a third question concerning free will, whether man has it. Luther replied, "This expression 'free will' was very odious to all the fathers, although they conceded, as we do too, that God gave man a free will. But the question here is whether this freedom is in our power. One ought properly call it a changeable, mutable will because God works in us and we are passive; like a potter, from the same material he can make a vessel either for honor or dishonor [Rom 9:21]. Accordingly, our free will is passive, not active, because it doesn't lie in our power."

Thereupon he instructed him [the student] to read the Bible and Philip's *Loci Communes*.[19]

---

17. Arius (*ca.* 256–336), one of the most notorious of heretics, was condemned by the Council of Nicaea (325) on account of his teaching about the person of Christ.
18. Roman emperor from A.D. 379 to 395.
19. Philip Melanchthon's *Loci communes rerum theologicarum* (Wittenberg, 1521), intended as a key to the interpretation of the Scriptures, was published in several editions and was expanded from an originally brief manual to a large book.

The Form of the Church Is a Servant Form

January 17, 1538

"Jerome Schurff and the philosophers are offended by the form of the church, which is subject to scandals and sects, because they think of the church as pure, holy, unspotted, and the dove of God. It's true that the church has this appearance in God's sight, but in the eyes of the world the church is like its bridegroom Christ: hacked to pieces, marked with scratches, despised, crucified, mocked [Isa 53:2, 3]. The image of the church and of Christ is a sheep. The image of hypocrites is a serpent, a viper, an adder. We're experiencing this in the very bitter hatred of religion which far exceeds every hatred of men and beasts. . . ."

Rejection of the Medieval Scholastics

February 2, 1538

On February 2 the elector of Saxony, Duke Henry of Saxony, the landgrave,[20] and Margrave Joachim[21] arrived in Wittenberg and did Luther the honor of asking him to preach the following day, which he did in praise of the Lord's Prayer. That evening Luther talked cheerfully with Amsdorf. They spoke at length about studies in the previous age, when the most gifted men had to occupy themselves with fruitless investigations. To students of our time the sophistical terminology of that age is altogether unfamiliar and seems barbarous. When the papacy was flourishing Scotus, Bonaventure, Gabriel, and Thomas had to embroider their thoughts with fantasies because they had no serious tasks to perform.

"Gabriel [Biel] wrote a book on the canon of the mass which I once thought was the best [on the subject]. When I read it, my heart bled. The authority of the Scriptures meant nothing to Gabriel. I still have the books that used to torment me so. Scotus wrote best on the third book of the *Sentences*. Occam was very clever in his devotion to method; he had a fondness for enlarging upon and amplifying

---

20. A count who had jurisdiction over a large territory in medieval Germany.
21. The military governor of a frontier province in medieval Germany.

things into infinity, but Thomas was most loquacious because he was seduced by metaphysics.

"God led us away from all this in a wonderful way; without my quite being aware of it he took me away from that game more than twenty years ago. How difficult it was at first when we journeyed toward Kemberg after All Saints' Day in the year 1517, when I first made up my mind to write against the crass errors of indulgences! Dr. Jerome Schurff advised against this: 'You wish to write against the pope? What are you trying to do? It won't be tolerated!' I replied, And if they have to tolerate it? Presently Sylvester, master of the sacred palace, entered the arena, fulminating against me with this syllogism: 'Whoever questions what the Roman church says and does is heretical. Luther questions what the Roman church says and does, and therefore [he is a heretic].' So, it all began.

"The pope speaks of the church in three distinct ways: essentially it is the body of the church itself, representatively it is the college of cardinals, virtually it is the pope himself. There is no mention of the council, for the pope wishes to be the virtual church, above the Scriptures and the authority of councils. Duke George is so zealous in behalf of the essential church because he wishes himself to be the church. He hates the pope, and so he wants to act as reformer of the church and reform him; as the bishop of Mainz should have only one bishopric and ride with fourteen horses, and as the bishop of Merseburg should ride with three horses, so the pope should cease from his acts of simony. For all the papists hold that the bishops should remain but should be reformed. However, the papists don't want to risk being found in error during a reform.

"Italy has often been humiliated before, but it has always been proud. Now, however, it is afraid and acknowledges its wickedness, but it doesn't wish to be punished by us Germans because we are a barbarous nation in its eyes. Nevertheless, if somebody were to arise in Italy who had authority and protection, he would be able to accomplish something."

The Mass Not of Primary Importance

February 2, 1538

Dr. Schneidewein said that on many points the Italians are Lutheran and would commend him [Luther] without hesitation. "If you had not attacked the mass," they said, "you would have a large following in Italy." To reject the mass is the most horrible thing in their eyes. They are so attached to this cultus that they think that anybody who has attended mass will on that day be free from danger and unable to sin. It is on this account that the greatest sins and murders occur after the hearing of masses; long lasting hate and feuds lead to homicide after mass. A certain man, who plotted against his enemy in hate and animosity for two years, was unable to catch up with him until he took him by surprise in church after mass, killed him, and fled.

Then Luther responded, "My book on the abrogation of the mass[22] is quite harsh. It was written against blaspheming opponents and not for beginners who are offended by it. If twenty years ago anybody had taken away the mass from me he would have had a fight on his hands with me, for at that time I adored it with my whole heart. And yet the mass and the entire papacy are based on nothing else than gain and profit."

Disjunction of Faith and Life Criticized

June 20, 1538

The wife of Duke Henry, prince of Freiberg, came to Wittenberg on June 20. Luther spoke with her twice about the arrogance and insolence of Dr. Jacob and admonished her to have regard for the offenses he was causing the church, etc. A councilman from Freiberg was also present [in Wittenberg] in order to call another man [as minister], and he reported Jacob's ungodly conduct and departure.[23] He said that Jacob had preached carnal license and had taught: "Do what you please. Only believe and you will be saved."

---

22. *The Misuse of the Mass* (1521).
23. Jacob Schenk (1508–1546) adopted antinomian views, and this led to his expulsion from Freiberg.

Luther replied, "This is a wicked disjunction. Turn the matter about: 'Dear fellow, believe in God, and then afterward, when you are reborn, are a new man, etc., do whatever comes to hand.' The fools don't know what faith is. They suppose it's just a lifeless idea. It's similar to what the sophists[24] taught about infused faith or unformed faith, which, they said, is a gift of the Holy Spirit even in infants and retains its place in mortal sin. In contrast, they said, there is a formed faith[25] which expresses itself in love and doesn't sin. Thus, they taught. However, it's impossible to be reborn of God and yet sin, for these two things contradict each other. Alas, dear God, many offenses will occur because we don't fear God and don't pray and presume, instead, to achieve something with the powers of our own nature."

A Parable on the Function of the Law

October 13, 1538

On October 13, he [Martin Luther] preached at home on the gospel, Luke 14 [:1–11], since he was unable to go to church. On that day, he marveled very much at the impudence of the antinomians, who reject the necessary teaching of the law so strongly and do not see its effect. Augustine[26] depicted the power and function of the law in a beautiful simile: Through the law the sins in us are made transparent and the wrath of God is increased. This is not the fault of the law but of our nature. It is like chalk stone, which is quiescent unless water is poured on it, when it becomes hot, not through the fault of the water but by virtue of its own nature. However, if oil is poured on the chalk, the chalk stays still and does not boil. This parable is excellent.

---

24. Scholastic theologians of the late Middle Ages.
25. Grace was thought of as a thing poured (infused) into man, when receptive, through the sacraments. Faith that was not formed by love was regarded as imperfect; faith formed by love was deemed perfect or sinless.
26. Augustine, *The City of God*, XXI, 4, 3.

Examples of the Faulty Proofs of the Papists

November 25, 1538

"Since the papists have a bad case they try to defend themselves with very defective arguments which don't prove anything. Their arguments should therefore be repudiated altogether. Here is an example: All praise is invocation; the saints should be praised; therefore, they should be invoked. I deny the major premise, for all praise is not invocation.

"Another example: Every act of concupiscence is illicit; the marital act is an act of concupiscence; therefore [marriage is illicit]. I reply to the minor premise: The marital act is not an act of concupiscence. Rather, the act which attracts sex to sex is a divine ordinance. Even if by mischance the act is impure on account of original sin, in itself it's still licit and pure.

"Still another example: The teaching of the forgiveness of sins is necessary; an indulgence is a remission of sins; therefore [the teaching of indulgences is necessary]. I reply: Indulgences are not the forgiveness of sins but satisfaction for the remission of penalties, and this is an invention."

Are We Rewarded in View of Our Works?

Between January 15 and 21, 1539

An Englishman asked Dr. Martin Luther about this question, which is very common in England: Whether godly persons who are already justified should expect some merit on account of the works that follow justification? Dr. Martin Luther replied, "It should be understood at the outset that we who are already justified are still sinners, and so we believe in and pray for forgiveness of sins in this life. 'Therefore, let everyone who is godly offer prayer to thee' [Ps 32:6]. 'Do not enter into judgment with your servant, [for no one living is righteous before you]' [Ps 143:2]. This is a certain statement. We're all sinners and live under the grace of the forgiveness of sins.

"In the second place, God promises reward to those who do works, and therefore we earn something, etc. Surely God gives works to individuals, but differently, as one star differs from another. Yet all of these are under the forgiveness of sins. As heaven (that is, justification) is under grace, so much the more are the stars. As the stars don't make heaven but only adorn it, so works don't merit heaven but only adorn justifying faith. This is the only reasoning that solves everything: 'I believe in Jesus Christ, who suffered under Pilate for us.' Everything is his; nothing is ours. Afterward, when by grace we are sons of God, we differ in our gifts, just as there are different stars in heaven.

"In short, the article of justification by Christ solves everything. If Christ merits it, we merit nothing. In Christ there are gifts, not merits. Likewise, since capital and substantial righteousness is nothing, how much less will accidental righteousness count in God's sight? Substantial righteousness is the righteousness of faith, but accidental righteousness is gifts, not merits. God crowns nothing but his own gifts, as Augustine said. He expounded the term 'merit' very well against the deceit of the sophists, who said that the Blessed Virgin merited becoming the mother of Christ, the Son of God, because of her virginity; that is, she was suited in her maidenly body to give birth to him. Truly, an excellent merit! It's as if somebody were to say, 'This tree merits the bearing of fruit because God ordained it to do so.' Surely, one should look upon God's gifts and ordinance, not upon our works. Thus, Augustine carefully reflected on the term 'merit' and concluded from the words of Mary, 'Here am I, the servant of the Lord' [Luke 1:38] and 'He has looked with favor on the lowliness of his servant' [Luke 1:48], that it depends on God's grace and not our merit. The merit of our works is nothing before God. The merit of our justification is grace, or Christ died in vain. Besides, we're all non-doers because there must be a diversity of gifts. This error comes from a confusion of the law and the gospel; when each of these teachings doesn't remain in its place and sphere, we turn heaven into hell and hell into heaven."

Belief in the Gospel Because of the Church?

April 6, 1539

"In the passage, 'I would not believe the gospel unless the authority of the church urged me to,' Augustine never wished to embrace the opinion of the papists. He didn't want to write what should be believed but what should be judged, as another passage indicates, 'I do not wish you to believe my writings more than the Holy Scriptures.' But the sophists poked fun at Paul for having written obscurely and confusedly. Ah, dear God, this treasure of the Holy Scriptures belongs only to a contrite heart and a humble and God-fearing spirit. The ungodly must be exposed and their boasting put down. This is what Stephen did in Acts 7 [:2–53], where he spoke against the place of Jerusalem, against the law, against the prosperous people, against a demanding God. Truly it was an excellent and sharp sermon! In the Roman church, today the glory of the church is not at all comparable with the glory of Jerusalem and of the people Israel."

The Faith that Justifies Is Not Knowledge

June 16, 1539

On June 16, there was an examination of candidates for ordination at which the proposition put for debate was: "Faith justifies; faith is a work; therefore, works justify." He [Martin Luther] responded, "Faith justifies not as a work, or as a quality, or as knowledge, but as assent of the will and firm confidence in the mercy of God. For if faith were only knowledge, then the devil would certainly be saved because he possesses the greatest knowledge of God and of all the works and wonders of God from the creation of the world. Accordingly, faith must be understood otherwise than as knowledge. In part, however, it is assent."

The Incarnation of Christ and the Trinity

May 16, 1540

"If anybody takes counsel with reason, he can't agree with our articles of faith. The Turk holds his people to their duty more by religion than by arms, for they believe that God is the almighty Creator of heaven and earth, that Christ is a prophet, that by civil uprightness they can merit heaven, etc.

"However, I have learned, not only through the Scriptures but also from severe inner struggles and trials, that Christ is God and has put on flesh, and likewise I have learned the doctrine of the Trinity. Today, therefore, I don't so much believe as I know through experience that these doctrines are true. In the worst temptations, nothing can help us but faith that God's Son has put on flesh, is bone [of our bone], sits at the right hand of the Father, and prays for us. There is no mightier comfort. From the beginning of the world God has defended this doctrine against all heretics, who are innumerable, and defends it today against the Turk and the pope. He always confirms it by miracles, allows us to call his Son the Son of God and true God, and hears us all when we call upon him in Christ's name.

"What will preserve us today in such great perils except prayer to Christ? If anybody should say that Master Philip or I or others will, he would lie to us. God does it for the sake of Christ, about whom the apostles preach today.... Accordingly, we'll abide by these articles, even against reason, for they have stood up and will stand."

The Place of Reason in the Christian Faith

Between May 21 and June 11, 1540

Severus said, "Doctor, the Jewish physician Ricius writes against our faith and is distressed that Philip wrote that articles of faith cannot be comprehended by reason...."

He [Martin Luther] responded, "Ah, what does reason understand? It can't comprehend how man is made from a drop of blood, how a cherry grows from a blossom, how bone and flesh came into existence. The world is full of everyday miracles, but, as Augustine said with reference to John 6 [:9], because they occur so often these things are deemed of little value. Christ once fed several thousand people with five loaves of bread. What does he do every day? But what happens daily is counted of little consequence. God produces wine from stones and makes butter and bread out of sand. So, he once formed man out of the ground,[27] and now he creates men every day out of drops of blood. There's no difference. Then he took a clod of earth in his hands and said, 'Be a man!' And today he says to the little drop, 'Be a man!' These are great miracles, but because of their frequency they are little esteemed.

"Who can understand anything about these things by means of reason? To be sure, enlightened reason can to some extent understand the Ten Commandments and the religion of the Jews; but articles of faith, like the Trinity and the incarnation of Christ—these don't tally with reason. Let's say that the king of France and a stone are the same thing, or this knife[28] and I are identical—these statements don't tally with reason. It's the same with the statement that God is man. We have to puzzle this out. I can reflect on it but can't understand it. Paul understood a good part of it, though he didn't comprehend all of it by any means. Yet he said with authority, 'In Christ are hid all the treasures of wisdom and knowledge' [Col 2:3]. For in this Christ all things, every creature, the whole Godhead are known. Here are united the greatest fortitude and the greatest weakness, life and death, righteousness and sin, the grace and the wrath of God. Ah, this is a high doctrine, but few care very much about it."

Predestination Cannot Be Searched Out

Between June 11 and 19, 1540

"I was troubled," said the doctor [Martin Luther], "by the thought of what God would do with me, but at length I repudiated such a thought and threw myself entirely on his revealed will. We can't do any better than that. The hidden will of God can't be searched out by man. God hides it on account of that very clever spirit, the devil, in order that he may be deceived. For he learned the revealed will from us, but God keeps the hidden will to himself. We have enough to learn about the humanity of Christ, in whom the Father revealed himself. But we are fools who neglect the revealed Word and the

---

27. Cf. Gen 2:7.
28. Luther, seated at table, probably had a knife in his hand.

will of the Father in Christ and, instead, investigate mysteries which ought only to be worshiped. As a result, many break their necks."

"He Hardens the Heart of Whomever He Wills"

Between June 11 and 19, 1540

Somebody asked [Martin Luther], "Is the hardening of the heart in the Scriptures[29] to be taken literally or figuratively?"

The doctor replied, "Literally, but not actively, because God doesn't do anything that's bad. Yet his omnipotence does everything, and as he finds man, so he acts on him. Pharaoh was by nature wicked; God acted on him, and Pharaoh continued to be wicked.[30] His heart was hardened because God didn't hinder Pharaoh's ungodly plans by his Spirit and grace. Why God didn't hinder them is not for us to ask. This 'why' destroys many souls when they search after that which is too high for us. God says, 'Why I am doing this you do not know, but ponder my Word, believe in Christ, pray, and I will make everything turn out well.' If God should be asked at the last judgment, 'Why did you permit Adam to fall?' and he answered, 'In order that my goodness toward the human race might be understood when I gave my Son for man's salvation,' we would say, 'Let the whole human race fall again in order that thy glory may become known! Because thou hast accomplished so much through Adam's fall we do not understand thy ways.'

"There is a threefold light: that of reason, that of grace, and that of glory."

Scholastics Taught Reliance on Oneself

Between August 7 and 24, 1540

"Scholastic theology agrees on this point, that man can merit grace *de congruo*[31] by his purely natural powers, and all the schoolmen taught at least this: 'Do what lies in your strength.' But Occam,

---

29. Cf. Rom 9:18.
30. Cf. Exod 7:13.
31. In scholastic theology merits of congruity may be secured by people in proportion to the good works they perform by their natural powers.

though he was superior to all the others in mental acumen and refuted all the rest of the positions, expressly said and taught that it isn't to be found in the Scriptures that the Holy Spirit is necessary for good works.

"These men had talent and leisure and grew old as they lectured, but they had no understanding at all of Christ because they despised the Bible and because nobody read the Bible for the sake of meditation but only for the sake of knowledge, as one would read a historical writing."

Plato and the Immortality of the Soul

Between September 2 and 17, 1540

The doctor [Martin Luther] said, "We are indeed poor people. We are poor and despised, as if it will remain so forever."

Then somebody said, "The heathen argued this way: It's bad for good people here; therefore, there's another life."

"Yes," said the doctor, "this is the best argument that all the heathen have. Plato's minor premise [to prove the immortality of the soul], that the soul is not made from the elements, and his proof (because our knowledge and such swift motion can't be the effect of elementary nature) don't stand up. Augustine disputed the matter vigorously and produced many facts in support of it, but even a sheep produces swift motion when it sees a wolf! Accordingly, their argument isn't adequate. But think of the Creator; this indicates the answer."

Luther Rejects the Pre-existence of the Soul

Between September 2 and 17, 1540

Hereupon somebody asked whether Plato's opinion about the soul is true.

"No, indeed!" replied the doctor. "How can Plato speak about this matter? I believe that God made the whole man from the dust of the earth, for the text [Gen 2:7] says that God made man. 'Man' doesn't mean the body alone but always means the body and the soul, and accordingly, the Scriptures call the soul 'the breath of life' [Gen 2:7].

Since the soul was in that instance made with the body, so when a child is born today the soul is created together with the body, contrary to Plato. Although all others disagree, it's my opinion that the soul isn't added from the outside but is created out of the matter of the semen. This is my reason: If the soul came from somewhere else, it would be made bad by contact with the body, but the soul isn't bad by chance but by nature. Consequently, the soul must be born out of corrupt matter and seed and must be created by God out of the matter of a man and a woman."

Classical Proofs for the Existence of God

Summer or Fall, 1542

"Aristotle is altogether epicurean. He doesn't believe that God cares about human affairs, or if he believes it, he thinks that God governs the world the way a sleepy maidservant rocks a child in a cradle. Cicero, on the other hand, made more progress. I think he collected every good thing that he found in all the Greek writers. The best argument that there is a God—and it often moved me deeply—is this one that he proves from the generation of species: a cow always bears a cow, a horse always bears a horse, etc. No cow gives birth to a horse, no horse gives birth to a cow, no goldfinch produces a siskin. Therefore, it is necessary to conclude that there is something that directs everything thus. We may be able to know very well that God exists from the sure and perpetual motion of the heavenly constellations—every year we find the sun rising and setting in its proper place—and likewise from the reliability of the seasons which give us winter and summer with such regularity. These things that happen every day are held to be unimportant and don't astonish us. But if one brought up a child from early childhood in a dark place and after twenty years brought him out, he would wonder about the sun, what it is, how it always adheres to a particular course, and how it moves according to a precise schedule of time. To us it is nothing because we pay little attention to what happens every day."

The Greatest Thing in Death Is Fear

September, 1542

"Fear of death is death itself and nothing else. Anybody who has torn death from deep down in his heart does not have death or taste it."

Somebody inquired about the pains of death, and Martin Luther replied, "Ask my wife if she felt anything when she was really dead."[32] She herself responded, "Nothing at all, Doctor."

Thereupon Dr. Martin Luther continued, "For this reason I say that the greatest thing in death is the fear of death. It is written in the Epistle to the Hebrews [2:9], 'that by the grace of God he might taste death for everyone.' We are blessed if we don't taste death, which is very bitter and sharp. How great the pain of tasting death is we can discern in Christ when he said, 'I am deeply grieved, even to death' [Matt 26:38]. I regard these as the greatest words in all the Scriptures, although it is also a great and inexplicable thing that Christ cried out on the cross, 'Eli, Eli,' etc. [Matt 27:46]. No angel comprehends how great a thing it was that he sweated blood [Luke 22:44]. This was tasting and fearing death. Creation consoles the Creator[33] and the disciples noticed nothing of these things," etc.

How One Can Become a Good Theologian

Winter of 1542–1543

"If anybody wishes to become a theologian, he has a great advantage, first of all, in having the Bible. This is now so clear that he can read it without any trouble. Afterward he should read Philip's *Loci Communes*. This he should read diligently and well, until he has its contents fixed in his head. If he has these two he is a theologian, and neither the devil nor a heretic can shake him. The whole of theology is open to him, and afterward he can read whatever he wishes for edification. If he wishes, he can read, in addition, Melanchthon's

---

32. The reference is to the grave illness of Luther's wife Katherine in 1540.
33. Cf. Luke 22:43.

Romans and my *Galatians* and *Deuteronomy*. These will give him the art of speaking and a copious vocabulary.

"There's no book under the sun in which the whole of theology is so compactly presented as in the *Loci Communes*. If you read all the fathers and sententiaries[34] you have nothing. No better book has been written after the Holy Scriptures than Philip's. He expresses himself more concisely than I do when he argues and instructs. I'm garrulous and more rhetorical.

"If my advice were taken, only the books of mine that contain doctrine would be printed, such as my *Galatians, Deuteronomy,* and *John*. The rest [of my books] should be read merely for the history, in order to see how it all began,[35] for it was not so easy at first as it is now."

Man Is a Whole and Not Merely Body or Soul

Winter of 1542–1543

Some said that after the soul has escaped from the mortal body, it immediately migrates to heaven, as Christ said, "Today you will be with me in Paradise" [Luke 23:43].

To this he [Martin Luther] responded, "Yes, what does this word 'today' mean? It's true that souls hear, feel and see after death, but how this occurs we don't understand. Where do those stay who hang on the gallows? If we try to figure this out according to [our conception of time in] this life, we're fools. Christ has given his answer, for his disciples were undoubtedly just as curious. [He said,] 'Those who believe in me, even though they die, will live' [John 11:25]. Similarly [Paul wrote], 'Whether we live or whether we die, we are the Lord's' [Rom 14:8]."

Before this he had said to his wife,[36] "Yes, you, too, are already in heaven. Christians, both those who are dead and those who are living, await a resurrection of the dead. Abraham lives too. God is God of the living [Matt 22:32]. Now, if one should say that Abraham's soul lives with God but his body is dead, this distinction is rubbish. I will

---

34. Late medieval commentators on Peter Lombard's *Four Books of Sentences.*
35. I.e., how the Reformation began.
36. This earlier conversation between Luther and his wife Katherine shifts the question from 'When does the soul go to heaven?' to 'Is the soul separated from the body at death?'

attack it. One must say, 'The whole Abraham, the whole man, shall live.' The other way you tear off a part of Abraham and say, 'It lives.' This is the way the philosophers speak: 'Afterward the soul departed from its domicile,' etc.[37] That would be a silly soul if it were in heaven and desired its body!"

Somebody observed that the dispute about the location of hell is similar, inasmuch as no certain place was assigned to the demons. Luther added, "The Scriptures say so. Peter declares in 2 Peter 2 [:4] that God cast them [the angels who sinned] into hell. There they don't suffer punishment as yet, although they are condemned. For if they were already punished, the devils wouldn't engage in so much knavery."

Then somebody said, "It is nevertheless asserted in the Creed, 'he descended into hell.'" Luther responded, "This must be believed. We can't understand it. That's the way it is. There will be debate about how the Trinity is in the unity (when there's no relation between the infinite and the finite), how nature can produce such a strange marvel as a God-man, etc. [While occupied thus with disputation] men will let the article concerning justification go. If only we would study in the meantime how to believe and pray and become godly! We're not content with that which we can understand and insist on disputing about something higher, which we can't possibly understand and which our Lord God doesn't want us to understand. That's the way human nature is. It wishes to do what is forbidden; the rest it ignores and then starts asking, Why? Why? Why? This is what happens when philosophy is introduced into theology. When the devil went to Eve with the question Why? the game was up. One should be on one's guard against this. It's better to fall on one's knees and pray an Our Father. This will help more.

"Dear Lord God, protect us from the devil, and also from ourselves!"

---

37. Luther seems not to have had any particular philosopher in mind here but to have referred to the interest which philosophers in general showed in the question of the immortality of the soul.

The Conscience Bears Witness and Accuses

Winter of 1542–1543

"Caiaphas didn't know that Christ is true God. This is so. But in the meantime, he knew this, that harm would be done to that man.[38] So the bishops also think that they are offering service to God[39] by killing Christians; yet they know that they ought not to kill those who are condemned for no cause. But our bishops take it to be nothing but trickery. They oppose what has been demonstrated to be true. William of Bavaria and the bishop of Mainz asked Eck at a meeting whether the things that we taught could be overturned by Holy Scripture, and Eck replied, 'They can't be overthrown by Holy Scripture but only by the teaching of the fathers and the councils.' They confess that we have the Scriptures [on our side], and yet they persecute us.

"At the same meeting the bishop of Mainz said, 'Dear lords, if they had no other article than the one about the marriage of priests, we would be lost, for we don't know how to maintain our position, and we can't.' The scoundrels see this very well, and yet they attack us. Nature teaches them that we are born male and female, and therefore they can't abolish marriage. However, marriage does not consist only of sleeping with a woman—everybody can do that—but keeping house and bringing up children must also be considered by anybody who intends to take a wife. So, the bishop of Salzburg also said against Master Philip, 'Why do you argue so much against priests? Priests have never been any good!' Thereupon Philip said, 'This is a matter of conscience.' The bishop then said, 'Are you going to talk a lot about conscience?' These were hard and wicked words. What kind of comfort can a man's poor, terrified conscience have if he doesn't believe anything about conscience? The only thing that concerns a poor sinner is his conscience. Well, then, God will find them out!

"A poor friar once went to Rome to secure a letter concerning a monastery from the pope. A cardinal who gave the letter to the friar demanded three thousand crowns, and the friar asked, 'Do you think

---

38. Cf. John 11:47–53.
39. Cf. John 16:2.

I'm God?' Then the cardinal (for he was not so bad) said that the friar should give thirty crowns, one tenth of the amount, and that it was necessary to give this. Thereupon the friar said, 'O Blessed Virgin Mary! Do you at Rome also have a conscience? The conscience is an evil beast who makes a man take a stand against himself.' He correctly defined conscience according to Paul in Romans 2 [:15]."

It Is Faith that Justifies, Not Works

Spring, 1543

"That works don't merit life, grace, and salvation is clear from this, that works are not spiritual birth but are fruits of this birth. We are not made sons, heirs, righteous, saints, Christians by means of works, but we do good works once we have been made, born, created such. So, it's necessary to have life, salvation, and grace before works, just as a tree doesn't deserve to become a tree on account of its fruit but a tree is by nature fitted to bear fruit. Because we're born, created, generated righteous by the Word of grace, we're not fashioned, prepared, or put together as such by means of the law or works. Works merit something else than life, grace, or salvation—namely, praise, glory, favor, and certain extraordinary things—just as a tree deserves to be loved, cultivated, praised, and honored by others on account of its fruit. Urge the birth and substance of the Christian and you will at the same time extinguish the merits of works insofar as grace and salvation from sin, death, and the devil are concerned.

"Infants who have no works are saved by faith alone, and therefore faith alone justifies. If the power of God can do this in one person it can do it in all, because it's not the power of the infant but the power of faith. Nor is it the weakness of the infant that does it, otherwise that weakness would in itself be a merit or be equivalent to one. We'd like to defy our Lord God with our works. We'd like to become righteous through them. But he won't allow it. My conscience tells me that I'm not justified by works, but nobody believes it. 'Against you, you alone, have I sinned and done what is evil in your sight, so that you are justified in your sentence and blameless when you pass judgment [Ps 51:4]. What is meant by 'forgive us our debts' [Matt

6:12]? I don't want to be good. What would be easier than for a man to say, 'I am a sinful man' [Luke 5:8]? But thou art a righteous God. That would be bad enough, but we are our own tormentors. The Spirit says, 'You are righteous' [Ps 119:137]. The flesh can't say this: 'you are justified in your sentence' [Ps 51:4]."

Love in Relation to Others, Faith to God

Spring, 1543

"In their books and writings, the sacramentarians have pestered us with 'love.' They say to us, 'You Wittenbergers have no love.' But if one asks, 'What is love?' we are told that it means to be united in doctrine and to stop religious controversies. Yes, do you hear? There are two tables [of the Decalogue], the first and the second. Love belongs in the second table. It's superior to all other works there. On the other hand, [in the first table] it is commanded: 'Fear God. Listen to his Word.' The sacramentarians don't bother with this. 'Whoever loves father or mother more than me is not worthy of me' [Matt 10:37], said Christ. You should have love for your parents, for your children. Love, love! Be good to your father and mother! However, 'whoever loves them more than me.' When this 'me' comes, love stops. Accordingly, I'm glad to be called obstinate, proud, headstrong, uncharitable, and whatever else they call me. Just so I'm not a participant [in their doctrine]. God keep me from that!"

6

Table Talks About Martin Luther

How Luther Handled Troublesome Thoughts

Summer or Fall, 1531

"When I'm troubled by thoughts which pertain to political questions or household affairs [said Martin Luther], I take up a psalm or a text of Paul and fall asleep over it. But the thoughts which come from Satan demand more of me. Then I have to resort to more difficult maneuvers before I extricate myself, although I easily get the upper hand in thoughts of an economic or domestic character. However, when I'm angry with God and ask him whether it's he or I who's wrong, then it's more than I can handle."

Luther's Evaluation of His Wife

Summer or Fall, 1531

"I wouldn't give up my Katy[1] for France or for Venice—first because God gave her to me and gave me to her; second, because I have often observed that other women have more shortcomings than

---

1. Luther was married to Katherine von Bora (1499–1552), a former nun, on June 13, 1525.

my Katy (although she, too, has some shortcomings, they are outweighed by many great virtues); and third, because she keeps faith in marriage, that is, fidelity and respect."

A wife ought to think the same way about her husband."

Luther's Own Call to the Ministry

Between November 9 and 30, 1531

"Unless those who are in the office of preacher find joy in him who sent them, they will have much trouble. Our Lord God had to ask Moses as many as six times.[2] He also led me into the office in the same way. Had I known about it beforehand, he would have had to take more pains to get me in. Be that as it may, now that I have begun, I intend to perform the duties of the office with his help. On account of the exceedingly great and heavy cares and worries connected with it, I would not take the whole world to enter upon this work now. On the other hand, when I regard him who called me, I would not take the whole world not to have begun it. Nor do I wish to have another God. Others before me, like Erasmus, criticized the life that people lived under the papacy, but I never thought I would be able to attack the two pillars on which the papacy rests, the mass and the [monastic] vows, for to do so seemed to me like an attack on God and his creation."

Luther's Early Study of the Bible

Between November 9 and 30, 1531

Once when he was a young man he [Martin Luther] happened upon a Bible. In it he read by chance the story about Samuel's mother in the Books of the Kings.[3] The book pleased him immensely, and he thought that he would be happy if he could ever possess such a book. Shortly thereafter he bought a postil; it also pleased him greatly, for

---

2. Cf. Exodus 3, 4.
3. Cf. 1 Sam 1:1–11.

it contained more Gospels[4] than it was customary to preach on in the course of a year.

When he became a monk, he gave up all his books. Shortly before this he had bought a copy of the *Corpus iuris*[5] and I do not know what else. He returned these to the bookseller. Besides Plautus[6] and Vergil[7] he took nothing with him into the monastery. There the monks gave him a Bible bound in red leather. He made himself so familiar with it that he knew what was on every page, and when some passage was mentioned he knew at once just where it was to be found.

"If I had kept at it," he said, "I would have become exceedingly good at locating things in the Bible. At that time, no other study pleased me so much as sacred literature. With great loathing I read physics, and my heart was aglow when the time came to return to the Bible. . . . I read the Bible diligently. Sometimes one important statement occupied all my thoughts for a whole day. Such statements appeared especially in the weightier prophets, and (although I could not grasp their meaning) they have stuck in my memory to this day. Such is the assertion in Ezekiel, 'I have no pleasure in the death of the wicked,' etc. [Ezek 33:11]."

Treatment of Melancholy, Despair, Etc.

November 30, 1531

"When I was in spiritual distress a gentle word would restore my spirit. Sometimes my confessor said to me when I repeatedly discussed silly sins with him, 'You are a fool. God is not incensed against you, but you are incensed against God. God is not angry with you, but you are angry with God.' This was magnificently said, although it was before the light of the gospel.[8] "Right here at this table, when the rest of you were in Jena, Pomeranus sometimes consoled me when I was sad by saying, 'No doubt God is thinking: What more can I

---

4. Appointed lections of the church year. A postil was a collection of sermons or commentaries on the appointed lessons of the church year.
5. The collection of canon law which he had intended to use in his study of law.
6. T. M. Plautus (d. 184 B.C.), a Roman writer of comedies.
7. Vergilius Maro (70–19 B.C.), a Roman poet.
8. Luther refers to his experience as a monk before the beginning of the Reformation.

do with this man? I have given him so many excellent gifts, and yet he despairs of my grace!' These words were a great comfort to me. As a voice from heaven they struck me in my heart, although I think Pomeranus did not realize at the time what he had said and that it was so well said.

"Those who are troubled with melancholy," he [Martin Luther] said, "ought to be very careful not to be alone, for God created the fellowship of the church and commanded brotherliness, as the Scriptures testify, 'Woe to one who is alone and falls,' etc. [Eccles 4:10]. To be gloomy before God is not pleasing to him, although he would permit us to be depressed before the world. He does not wish me to have a long face in his presence, as he says, 'I have no pleasure in the death of the wicked' [Ezek 33:11] and 'Rejoice in the Lord' [Phil 4:4]. He desires not a servant who does not expect good things of him.

"Although I know this, I am of a different mind ten times in the course of a day. But I resist the devil, and often it is with a fart that I chase him away. When he tempts me with silly sins, I say, 'Devil, yesterday I broke wind too. Have you written it down on your list?' When I say to him, 'You have been put to shame,' he believes it, for he does not want to be despised. Afterward, if I engage him in further conversation, I upbraid him with the pope and say, 'If you do the same as he does, who is your pope that I should celebrate him? Look what an abomination he has prepared, and it continues to this day!' Thus, I remind myself of the forgiveness of sin and of Christ and I remind Satan of the abomination of the pope. This abomination is so great that I am of good cheer and rejoice, and I confess that the abomination of the papacy after the time of Christ is a great consolation to me. Consequently, those who say that one should not rebuke the pope are dreadful scolds. Go right ahead and inveigh against the pope, especially if the devil disturbs you about justification. He often troubles me with trivialities. I don't notice this when I'm depressed, but when I feel better I recognize it easily.

"Well, then, our furious foe has done us much harm. I know that I shall see him and his flaming missiles in the last day. As long as we have pure teaching he will not harm us, but if the teaching is wrong we are done for. But praise be to God, who gave us the Word and also allowed his only Son to die for us! He did not do this in vain. Accordingly, we should entertain the hope that we are saints, that we are saved, and that this will be manifest when it is revealed. Since Christ accepted the thief on the cross[9] just as he was and received Paul after all his blasphemies and persecutions,[10] we have no reason to despair. As a matter of fact, all of us must be saved just as the thief and Paul were. Good God, what do you think it means that he has given his only Son? It means that he also offers whatever else he possesses. We have no reason, therefore, to fear his wrath, although we must continue to fear on account of the old Adam, who is still unable to understand this as it ought to be understood. If we had only the first three words of the Creed, 'I believe in God the Father,' they would still be far beyond our understanding and reason. In short, it does not occur to man that God is Father. If it did, man could not live for a single moment. Accordingly, in this infirm flesh we must have faith, for if we were capable of fully believing, heaven would already be here. There is therefore no reason to fear, in so far as the object of fear is concerned, and yet we cannot understand and are compelled on account of the weakness of our flesh to suffer assaults of fear and desperation. Thus, the catechism remains lord,[11] and there is nobody who understands it. I am accordingly compelled to pray it every day, even aloud, and whenever I happen to be prevented by the press of duties from observing my hour of prayer, the entire day is bad for me. Prayer helps us very much and gives us a cheerful heart, not on account of any merit in the work, but because we have spoken with God and found everything to be in order.

"Having been taught by experience I can say how you ought to restore your spirit when you suffer from spiritual depression. When you are assailed by gloom, despair, or a troubled conscience you should eat, drink, and talk with others. . . ."

---

9. Cf. Luke 23:39–43.
10. Cf. Gal 1:13.
11. I.e., the catechism (e.g., Luther's *Small Catechism*), which contains the Creed and an explanation of it.

Luther Drinks to God's Honor

Between November 30 and December 14, 1531

"If our Lord God can pardon me for having crucified and martyred him for about twenty years [by saying mass], he can also approve of my occasionally taking a drink in his honor. God grant it, no matter how the world may wish to interpret it!"

Luther Is Occupied with Many Duties

Between December 14, 1531 and January 22, 1532

"I am very busy. Four persons are dependent on me, and each of them demands my time for himself. Four times a week I preach in public, twice a week I lecture, and in addition I hear cases,[12] write letters, and am working on a book for publication. It is a good thing that God came to my aid and gave me a wife. She takes care of domestic matters, so that I do not have to be responsible for these too."

Luther's Analysis of Himself

End of March, 1532

"I am free from avarice, my age and bodily weakness protect me from sensual desire, and I am not afflicted with hate or envy toward anybody. Up to now only anger remains in me, and for the most part this is necessary and just. But I have other sins that are greater."

Luther "Excommunicated" Three Times

Between April 7 and 15, 1532

"Three times have I been excommunicated. The first time was by Dr. Staupitz, who absolved me from the observance and rule of the Augustinian Order so that, if the pope pressed him to imprison me or command me to be silent, he could excuse himself on the ground that I was not under his obedience. The second time was by the pope

---

12. Matrimonial cases.

and the third time was by the emperor.[13] Consequently, I cannot be accused of laying aside my habit, and I am now silent by divine authority alone."

God Must Be a Devout Man

Between April 7 and 15, 1532

"Our Lord God must be a devout man to be able to love knaves. I can't do it, although I am myself a knave."

Do Not Debate with Satan When Alone

Spring, 1533

"Almost every night when I wake up the devil is there and wants to dispute with me. I have come to this conclusion: When the argument that the Christian is without the law and above the law doesn't help, I instantly chase him away with a fart. The rogue wants to dispute about righteousness although he is himself a knave, for he kicked God out of heaven and crucified his Son. No person should be alone when he or she opposes Satan. The church and the ministry of the Word were instituted for this purpose, that hands may be joined together and one may help another. If the prayer of one doesn't help, the prayer of another will."

The Revolt and the Prophecy of John Huss

Spring, 1533

"Alexander III[14] published indulgences and ordered the angels to take away the souls of those who had died on the journey to Rome. John Huss[15] said at the time that this was avarice. He was accordingly summoned to Rome, but he sent his deputies there, and afterward a council was called. So, the cause of Huss is also mine. He rebelled against the indulgence for St. Peter's Church, and in the year 1415

---

13. At the Diet of Worms in 1521, Luther was declared an outlaw of the empire.
14. Pope from 1409 to 1410.
15. John Huss (1369–1415), Bohemian reformer, was burned at the stake during sessions of the Council of Constance.

he was put to death. His opposition lasted only two years. 'In another hundred years,' he said, 'you will have to pay attention and you won't be able to stop it.'"

As a Monk Luther Observed Prayers Strictly

Spring, 1533

"When I was a monk I was unwilling to omit any of the prayers,[16] but when I was busy with public lecturing and writing I often accumulated my appointed prayers for a whole week, or even two or three weeks. Then I would take a Saturday off, or shut myself in for as long as three days without food and drink, until I had said the prescribed prayers. This made my head split, and as a consequence I couldn't close my eyes for five nights, lay sick unto death, and went out of my senses. Even after I had quickly recovered and I tried again to read, my head went 'round and 'round. Thus, our Lord God drew me, as if by force, from that torment of prayers. To such an extent had I been captive [to human traditions]! . . .

"When Christ is away the devil is present and says, 'You must do it to the very last detail.' But Christ overlooks all sins. God gives so that we may be thankful. He never bothers me about my having done wrong in my teaching, but this is unknown to those who were in monasteries a long time. . . . For the devil can find a person quickly, especially if Christ is not in his heart. The devil leads such a person into the Holy Scriptures without Christ, that is, to the law and to works. So, it takes toil and trouble before Christ himself helps again."

One Should Not Pay Too Much Attention to Dreams

Spring, 1533

"This is where dreams come from. Man's spirit can't rest, for Satan is there even when a man is asleep, though angels are also present. The devil can so frighten me that sweat pours from me in my sleep.

"I don't pay attention to either dreams or signs. I have the Word, and that I let suffice. I don't want an angel to come to me. I wouldn't

---

16. Horary prayers, or prayers prescribed for monks at certain hours of the day.

believe him now anyway, although the time may come when I would desire it in special circumstances. I don't say that dreams and signs are of value at other times, nor do I care, for we already have everything we should have in the Scriptures. Troubled dreams are of the devil, because everything that serves death and terror and murder and lies is the devil's handiwork.

"Satan has often distracted me from prayer and has put such thoughts into my head that I ran away from it. The most severe bouts I have had with him I had when I was in bed at my Katy's side."

Luther Worries over Results of His Teaching

Spring, 1533

"'The devil has often troubled me by saying, 'Who commanded you to teach against the monasteries?' Or again, 'Before there was glorious peace, but now you have disturbed it, and who ordered you to do so?'" Here I interrupted his talk and said, "You didn't tell anybody either to leave the monastery or to disturb the peace. You only taught that it is in vain that people worship God with the precepts of men.[17] Then those things of which you have now spoken followed of their own accord under God's direction."

But he answered me thus, "Dear fellow, before it would have occurred to me to put it in this light I would have sweated anxiously over it."

Father Criticizes Luther for Becoming Monk

Fall, 1533

He [Martin Luther] became a monk against the will of his father. When he celebrated his first mass and asked his father why he was angry about the step he took, the father replied reproachfully, "Don't you know that it's written, Honor your father and your mother?" [Exod 20:12]. When he excused himself by saying that he was so frightened by a storm that he was compelled to become a monk, his

---

17. Cf. Matt 15:9.

father answered, "Just so it wasn't a phantom you saw!" Afterward it was his father who advised him to get married. . . .

Entrance on New Year with Expectation of End

January 1, 1532
In this year, 1532, Luther was forty-eight years old and he said, "I have another year to preach, but I am afraid I won't live so long. I hope I'll experience the last day. Know that it's at the door. Then what is written will happen: 'He will wipe every tear' [Rev 21:4]."

What If Your Teaching Should Be false?

Between January 1 and March 23, 1532
"Satan often said to me, 'What if your teaching by which you've overthrown the pope, the mass, and the monks should be false?' He often assailed me in such a way as to make me break out in sweat. Finally, I answered, 'Go and speak with my God, who commanded us to listen to this Christ.' Christ must do everything. Accordingly, we wish to be Christians and leave it to Christ to answer for this."

A Dead Luther May Give More Trouble

Between April 7 and May 1, 1532
"When I die, I want to be a ghost and pester the bishops, priests, and godless monks so that they have more trouble with a dead Luther than they could have had before with a thousand living ones."

In His Illness Luther Thinks of Death

Between April 7 and May 1, 1532
"One of these days, before I know it, I'll pass away," [Martin Luther said]. Philip said, "God will help, so that you will get well again." To this the doctor replied, "The Lord God has more trouble on his hands to devise a way of raising me up from the dead than I have to worry about dying."

Luther Leaves His Debts to His Wife

Between April 7 and May 1, 1532

"I'm rich," said Luther. "My God has given me a nun and has added three children. I don't worry about my debts, for when my Katy has paid them there will be more."

Luther Jests with His Wife About Monogamy

Between April 7 and May 1, 1532

[Martin Luther said,] "The time will come when a man will take more than one wife."

The doctor's wife responded, "Let the devil believe that!"

The doctor said, "The reason, Katy, is that a woman can bear a child only once a year while her husband can beget many."

Katy responded, "Paul said that each man should have his own wife" [1 Cor 7:2].

To this the doctor replied, "Yes, 'his own wife' and not 'only one wife,' for the latter isn't what Paul wrote."

The doctor spoke thus in jest for a long time, and finally the doctor's wife said, "Before I put up with this, I'd rather go back to the convent and leave you and all our children."

Luther's Account of His First Mass as Priest

May 20, 1532

"Christ must be a better man than Philip [Melanchthon] or Pomeranus to be able to make us such a gift, that we have offered him thus as a sacrifice."

When all the others had left, he stood with me in the court and said to me, "When I was about to hold my first mass, my father sent twenty gulden for food and came with twenty persons, all of whom he put up. Somebody said to him, 'You must have a good friend here that you should come to visit him with such a large company.'

"When at length I stood before the altar and was to consecrate, I was so terrified by the words *aeterno vivo vero Deo*[18] that I thought of running away from the altar and said to my prior, 'Reverend Father,

I'm afraid I must leave the altar. 'He shouted to me, 'Go ahead, faster, faster!'

"So terrified was I by those words! Already I had forebodings that something was wrong, but God didn't give me an understanding of this until later."

Luther's Parents Were Poor and Worked Hard

Between January 2 and 26, 1533
"In his youth, my father was a poor miner. My mother carried all her wood home on her back. It was in this way that they brought us up."

Luther Spends More Than He Receives

Between January 26 and 29, 1533
"God is the guardian and steward of the poor. I know this for certain from my experience, for I spend far more than I get from my stipend. So far, I've not written anything, lectured, or preached for compensation. The two hundred gulden that I get from the prince[19] I have and receive by his indulgence. He who has Christ has enough. I have not wanted to do anything for money, although I might have become rich. I wanted to scrape the money together," etc.

Luther Disparages His Earliest Writings

Between October 27 and December 4, 1536
When he [Martin Luther] heard that his books were in the library of the prince he said, "My books ought by no means to be placed in that library, especially not the earliest books which I wrote at the beginning, for they are offensive not only to my adversaries but also to me."

---

18. Latin: 'to Thee, the eternal, living, and true God.' Part of the canon of the mass.
19. Elector John Frederick of Saxony (1532–1547) gave Luther the annual gift he here refers to in addition to the house (the former Black Cloister) in which he lived.

Preparation for Baptism of Son Paul

January 29, 1533

"Gracious Lord,[20] I wish to impose on Your Grace once more. A son was just born to me, and I am a father again. Please help the poor fellow get where he belongs.[21] He was born the first hour during the night of January 28 in the year 1533, and he was named Paul. I've had him named Paul because St. Paul furnished me with many a good passage and argument, and so I wish to honor him by naming a son after him. God grant my son grace! . . ."

Gravely Ill, Luther Prepares for His Death

February, 1537

When Philip looked at him [Martin Luther][22] he was dissolved in tears, and Luther said, "John Loeser is accustomed to speak thus, 'It's no art to drink good wine, but to be able to drink bad wine is a real art.' So now you are thinking of teaching me to practice this art in order that I may be able to accept with resignation these pains of mine and this despair of life. If we accept good from the Lord's hands, why don't we submit to evil?[23] The Lord gave, and the Lord has taken away; blessed be the name of the Lord.[24] Long enough now have I played this game against the pope and the devil, and the Lord has wonderfully protected and comforted me. Why shouldn't I now bear with equanimity what he does with me according to his will? In any case our death is nothing compared with the death of the Son of God. Besides, so many very saintly men have been buried before us whose company we are not worthy of; if we desire to be with them, as we really do desire, it's necessary that we die. We ought to reach out for this with an eager spirit because our Lord is the Lord of life who holds us in his hand.

---

20. Hans Loeser, marshal of the elector of Saxony, was here asked to be a sponsor at Luther's son's baptism. It appears that this piece was dictated by Luther as a note to Loeser.
21. I.e., by baptism into the fellowship of the church.
22. While in Smalcald to attend a meeting of the Smalcald League, Luther had become gravely ill with a kidney stone.
23. Cf. Job 2:10.
24. Cf. Job 1:21.

"Of course, a great change has taken place as far as I am concerned: Yesterday I was quite resolute in spirit and strong in body, while today, as you see, I am pitiably broken in my strength. How much I am changed from what I was yesterday! Yesterday I felt exuberant and light as a bird. But, O God, we are nothing, and all that is ours is nothing, even when we are everything! I might have prayed to our Lord God, or at least grumbled at him, that he'd let me die in the land of my prince.[25] But if that's not to be, I'll be ready at whatever hour and place the Lord calls me. I'll be and I'll die an enemy of all the enemies of my Christ, and if I die under the excommunication of the pope may he himself also die under the ban of my Christ."

The next day—that is, on February 26—he said when he vomited as a result of his sickness, "Ah, dear Father, take this dear soul into thy hand. I give thee thanks and bless thee, and let all thy creatures bless thee. Grant that I may speedily be gathered to the fathers."

Later, when the vomiting ceased, he said, "Go, my dear soul, go in God's name. How poor and wretched we human beings are! I have almost no strength left, and yet how Satan troubles and disturbs what little strength I have! Give me constancy and patience in thy faithfulness, my Father, that I may overcome [Satan].

"To you, my dear Amsdod, I commend Katy, my wife. I have no doubt that Satan produces and sharpens these pains. There's an obstruction in my body that prevents the stone and urine from following their course. But by God's grace I'll have it better after this life. So, nothing that I now suffer from the devil will hurt me. I'll gladly go to pieces; only let Satan not have his way in the church after my death. I'm very much afraid of this because contempt of the gospel and ingratitude toward it are so great."

Hereupon he shed many bitter tears, sighed deeply, and folded his hands amid many sobs. "I'm concerned," he said, "lest the precious gospel may be lost, for it seems to me that I now observe some who first fall into strife and then yield to passions and forget that which is the chief thing in doctrine, with the result that the Word and the glory of God are lost to sight. How hard it became for us under the papacy! We read and did everything, and yet we found nothing. The

---

25. In the land of Elector John Frederick of Saxony.

more we looked, the further we were from our goal. I'm afraid the same thing will happen after I'm gone. The world doesn't care, but the pope knows that all his [utterances] are lies and trumpery."

At this point he again wept copiously [and continued], "Dear God, I am thy little creature, and thou art the Creator. I am thy clay, and thou art my potter.[26] If only the end will come for me and thou mayest preserve the Word longer! But I have reason to fear the opposite. I observe that the more we are enlightened, the more we suffer."

Then he sipped some almond broth and said, "Dear God, may it be blest for me either in time or for eternity! If this illness lasts longer, I'll surely go mad. Even if this should happen, I know that my God remains skillful and wise. Good God, how subject to death this wretched little body is! Except that I have faith in Jesus Christ, it wouldn't be surprising if I took my own life with a sword. The devil hates me, and so he increases my pain. He's got me in his claws, and no doubt I've deserved this from him. But avenge thyself, O Christ, against thy foe! I've done right to pick the pope to pieces, and I must hold him in check now once more. If anything good is to come of it, this should be done not in order that my health may be restored but in order that the power of the devil may be smashed forever. It hurts us, but God doesn't forsake us; he renders to each according to his works. So, let God only take me away, and pay the devil as he has deserved. Amen."

On the same day, he [Martin Luther] spoke as follows in the presence of Ponikau, a nobleman and chamberlain of the elector: "I'm obliged to be stoned to death like Stephen and to give the pope an occasion for pleasure, but I hope he won't laugh very long. My epitaph shall remain true: 'While alive I was your plague, when dead I'll be your death, O pope.'"[27]

Afterward he gave thanks to God for preserving him in the faith and confession of God's Word and name. Finally, he asked Ponikau to commend his [Luther's] wife and children to the prince and to thank the prince for his kindness.

---

26. Cf. Isa 29:16.
27. Cf. Acts 7:54–60. Luther makes a play on words with the stones that struck and killed Stephen and the kidney stones that were causing him pain internally.

The next day he said the same to the prince himself. First, he committed to him the care of the church and afterward the care of his home. On that occasion, the prince said that he hoped our Lord God would not do such a bad thing to his land and people [as to allow Luther to die], but if he did die, he promised to take care of the doctor's wife and children as if they were his own. He [Martin Luther] ordered the ministers to report the following to the chancellor of the duke of Saxony: "Tell my good friend the chancellor that I wish he might learn to know the pope as well as I know him. Then he'll be as hostile to him as I am." He raised himself up and, after making the sign of the cross with his hand, he said to us who were standing around him, "The Lord fill you with his benediction and with hatred of the pope!"

A Response to the Calling of the Council

March 19, 1537

When asked what reply he had given to the pope and the emperor with reference to the council,[28] he [Martin Luther] responded, "Nothing but intrigues are set up against us. The pope ordered the council to oppose the harmful Lutheran heresy and summons us to kiss the emperor's sword that slays us. Thus, we are called upon to surrender our own life and blood and concede that they are right. Surely this is too insolent and too much! It exceeds all imagination and utterance. Well, then, we'll defend ourselves with an Our Father and the Creed, but by no means with the Decalogue, for we're too weak in that. It isn't good. . . ."

Luther's Experience at His First Mass

Between March 21 and 28, 1537

"I, Martin Luther entered the monastery against the will of my father and lost favor with him, for he saw through the knavery of the monks very well. On the day on which I sang my first mass he said to me, 'Son, don't you know that you ought to honor your father?

---

28. The council called to convene in Mantua in 1537.

Just so it wasn't a phantom you saw!' Later when I stood there during the mass and began the canon,[29] I was so frightened that I would have fled if I hadn't been admonished by the prior. For when I read the words, 'Thee, therefore, most merciful Father,' etc., and thought I had to speak to God without a Mediator, I felt like fleeing from the world like Judas. Who can bear the majesty of God without Christ as Mediator? In short, as a monk I experienced such horrors; I had to experience them before I could fight them."

Luther's Illness and Comment on Medicine

Between March 28 and May 27, 1537

Dr. Martin [Luther] left the church when he felt faint during communion, and on his way he said, "Yesterday I felt fine, but today my condition is completely changed. It is due to change in the weather. Men are the best and most natural mathematicians, for they quickly feel in their limbs any opposition or conjunction [of stars] and any change of weather.

"The devil's also a fellow who can cause sickness. As Peter said in the book of Acts, the sick are oppressed by the devil [Acts 10:38]. Disease doesn't spring only from men's constitutions, and we observe that various medicines have been found to treat one sickness. Although these medicines have helped once or twice, soon they are ineffective. So, powerful is the devil that he can alter all medicines and drugs and change what's in the boxes. Accordingly, let us pray to the true physician, Christ. When the hour comes, as it must, in which we breathe our last breath, God grant that we may have a cheerful end. Amen."

Response to a False Report of His Death

Between May 27 and June 18, 1537

A certain messenger came from Hall, in the valley of the Inn in the Alps. He informed Dr. Martin [Luther] about a very common rumor

---

29. The canon of the mass, the central action of the Roman sacrament in which bread and wine were believed to be transubstantiated and offered to God as a sacrifice, was said inaudibly by the priest.

in Italy, which is received with joy by the papists, to the effect that Martin Luther was dead and buried and that his epitaph was written in Hebrew, Greek, and Latin letters. Many godly people were saddened by this rumor, the messenger said, and requested him to bring them a copy of the epitaph. "Since I find Your Reverence still alive," he said, "I beg you to give me a letter from your grave in order that with it I may comfort the godly people who have been grieving."

Dr. Martin [Luther] smiled and said, "This is an extraordinary request. Never before in my life have I written anything from my grave!" Nevertheless, he wrote the following lines: "I, Dr. Martin Luther, testify herewith in my own hand that I am of one mind with the devil, the pope, and all my enemies, for they wish to rejoice over my death. I begrudge them their joy from the bottom of my heart and would willingly have died in Smalcald, but God was not yet ready to sanction such joy. He will do this, however, sooner than they think, and it will be their misfortune, for they will then say, 'Would that Luther were still alive!' This is a transcript in German, Greek, Latin, and Hebrew from my grave."

Luther Recalls His Illness in Smalcald

February 5, 1538

On February 5 Luther spoke about the perilous times and sighed: "Dear God, if I had died of stone in Smalcald I would now have been in heaven, freed from all evil, for a year. I was at that time sufficiently annoyed by the physicians. They gave me as much to drink as if I had been a big ox. They worked over my body until all my members, even my private parts, became lifeless. I had to obey the physicians. I did what I did from necessity, lest I appear to neglect my body. Wretched is the man who relies on the help of physicians. I don't deny that medicine is a gift of God and I don't reject this knowledge, but where are the physicians who are perfect? A good regimen is worth a great deal. So, if I feel tired and nevertheless adhere to my regimen, go to bed by the ninth hour, and have a restful night, I will be refreshed. When I get up from my rest I can't work very long. My time has just about come anyhow."

Proposal to Publish Luther's Works

March 29, 1538

On March 29, the Strassburgers asked for permission to publish the collected works of Luther with a reliable index to the same. Luther replied, "I'd like all my books to be destroyed so that only the sacred writings in the Bible would be diligently read. For one is referred from one book to another, as it happened in the ancient church, when one turned from a reading of the Bible to a reading of Eusebius, then of Jerome, then of Gregory, and finally of the scholastics and philosophers. This will happen to us too. I'd like them [my books] to be preserved for the sake of history, in order that men may observe the course of events and the conflict with the pope, who once seemed formidable but is now regarded with disdain."

A Prince Invites Luther to Hunt

April 3, 1538

In the evening the prince of Anhalt, as deputy of the elector, invited Luther to join him in the hunt the following day and then to have supper with him. Luther replied, "I have indeed been sent here for this purpose, but I'm not a hunter of wild game. I give chase to the pope, the cardinals, the bishops, the canons, and the monks."

Hard Work Can Make a Man Old

April 19, 1538

The conversation then turned to Martin Bucer, who as a result of his very great cares and endless labors has grown old, although he is not yet fifty years old. Luther responded, "What one thinks can very well make a person old, and so can work. I used to work too. Often, I preached four sermons on one day. During the whole of one Lent I preached two sermons and gave one lecture every day. This was when I first preached on the Ten Commandments to a large congregation, for to preach on the catechism was then a new and uncommon thing."

Luther Recalls Proceedings in Augsburg

April 27, 1538

Then he [Martin Luther] began to tell of the proceedings at Augsburg [in 1518], how he was treated by the cardinal:[30] "When I was cited I went, but with strong legal protection from the elector and with recommendations to the Augsburgers, who with great diligence shielded me from conversation with the Italians, whom I was not to trust, for I didn't know them then. For three full days, I was in Augsburg without imperial escort. Meanwhile an Italian came to me now and then, summoned me to the cardinal, and urged me to recant: 'Say only one word, *Revoco*,[31] then the cardinal will commend you to the pope and you will return with glory to your prince.'

"After three days had passed, the bishop of Trent, in the name of the emperor, showed the cardinal my safe-conduct. Then I went to the cardinal as a suppliant. First, I fell on my knees; second, I lay down on the ground; and third, I stretched out in a prostrate position. Only after the cardinal had ordered me three times to arise, did I get up humbly. This greatly pleased the cardinal, and he hoped for a prompt victory. But when, after another day, I was unwilling to recant anything, he said, 'Do you think the pope cares about Germany? Do you imagine that the princes will defend you with arms?'

"'No.'

"'Where will you stay?'

"'Under the sky.'

"Such was the insolence of the pope. This is why his honor and majesty are despised. To him this is more bitter than death, but it can no longer be prevented.

"Then the pope humbled himself in a measure and wrote to the elector, even to Spalatin[32] and Pfeffinger,[33] asking them to hand me over and see to the execution of his command. To the elector, he wrote the following declaration: 'Although I do not know you per-

---

30. Cardinal Cajetan gave Luther a hearing in Augsburg in 1518, shortly after the start of the indulgence controversy.
31. Latin: 'I recant.'
32. George Spalatin, the elector's secretary.
33. Degenhart Pfeffinger was the elector's collector of revenues.

sonally, I did see your father Ernest in the city [of Rome]. He was a very obedient son of the church and attended our services with great devotion. I wish that Your Serenity would follow in his footsteps.'

"However, the elector marked well the unaccustomed humility of the pope, his bad conscience, and the fact that he was afraid. The elector also recognized the efficacy of the Scriptures, for my *Explanations*[34] circulated through all Europe in a very few days. So, the elector was strengthened in his decision not to carry out the pope's command, and he submitted to the judgment of the Scriptures.

"If the cardinal had acted more modestly in Augsburg and had accepted me as a suppliant, things would never have gone so far, for at that time I still knew little of the errors of the pope. If he had kept quiet, I would probably have kept quiet too. It was the Roman style, in an obscure and inexplicable case, for the pope to say, 'By papal authority we shall reserve this case for ourselves and shall eradicate it altogether.' Then both parties would have been compelled to keep silent. I think the pope would give three cardinals if the matter were back in the condition in which it was then."

Why the Lectures on Genesis Are Poor

May 29, 1538

Somebody referred to the lectures on Genesis and said that it would be desirable and useful to have them published. Luther replied, "The lectures are hastily thrown together and are imperfect. In them I offer others a stimulus to further reflection. Accordingly, it wouldn't be prudent to make them public. They are too poor. A single work like this demands the whole of a man. I'm too busy for it. I can't do justice to such a thing while I'm busy with many tasks. To do much and to do it well don't fit together. A person who is occupied with many tasks can't give his undivided attention to any one thing. Cicero complained that he couldn't easily recover a train of thought once it had been interrupted. It's a wretched business in this life! Those who live in idleness and riches are unwilling to do anything, and the oth-

---

34. The *Explanations* (1518) were an exhaustive explanation by Luther of his *Ninety-Five Theses*.

ers are kept from accomplishing anything by their poverty and preoccupation with many tasks."

Luther Faces His Illness with Resignation

July 17, 1538

On July 17, Luther was still suffering greatly. He was aware of the irregularity of his pulse and was consoled by the physician. He [Luther] responded, "I'm subject to the will of God. I've given myself up to him altogether. He'll take care of everything. I'm sure that he won't die because he is himself life and resurrection. Whoever lives and believes in him shall not die; though he die, yet shall he live [John 11:25]. Therefore, I submit to his will."

Another Account of the "Tower Experience"

September 12, 1538

"That expression 'righteousness of God' was like a thunderbolt in my heart When under the papacy I read, 'In your righteousness deliver me' [Ps 31:1] and 'in your truth,' I thought at once that this righteousness was an avenging anger, namely, the wrath of God. I hated Paul with all my heart when I read that the righteousness of God is revealed in the gospel [Rom 1:16, 17]. Only afterward, when I saw the words that follow—namely, that it's written that the righteous shall live through faith [Rom 1:17]—and in addition consulted Augustine, was I cheered. When I learned that the righteousness of God is his mercy, and that he makes us righteous through it, a remedy was offered to me in my affliction.

"But our antinomian friends wish in their folly to flatter secure men and to make them good by reminding them of righteousness, though such an age as ours is incapable of being terrified by the lightning of the law. On account of the great sense of security it's necessary to thunder and lightning with the law, for farmers and burghers are so ungodly that they don't take care of a single pastor. If the princes and lords didn't provide, we wouldn't last very long. Therefore, Isaiah put it well when he said, 'Kings shall be your foster fathers'

[Isa 49:23]. The farmers won't do it, as, alas, we see today from experience with these ungrateful people."

Proposal to Publish Luther's Collected Works

September 29, 1538

Men [printers] in Augsburg and Wittenberg urged Luther to allow them to publish his collected works. He replied, "I'll never consent to this proposal of yours. I'd rather that all my books would disappear and the Holy Scriptures alone would be read. Otherwise we'll rely on such writings and let the Bible go. Brenz wrote such a big commentary on twelve chapters of Luke that it disgusts the reader to look into it. The same is true of my commentary on Galatians. I wonder who encourages this mania for writing! Who wants to buy such stout tomes? And if they're bought, who'll read them? And if they're read, who'll be edified by them?"

The First Mass of a Priest Was an Occasion

December 5, 1538

"The first mass was an occasion for great profit [Martin Luther said]. It was a real time for snaring money by means of fees and presents. The canonical hours were then supplanted for the bridegroom by torches.[35] Amid the weeping of the spectators the young priest had to have the first dance with his mother, if she was living,[36] as Christ danced with his mother. When I celebrated my first mass in Erfurt I almost died because no faith was there. I reflected only on the dignity of my person, that I wasn't a sinner, that I shouldn't leave anything out."

---

35. The newly-ordained priest was married to the church. Hence, he was looked upon as a bridegroom and there were wedding torches.
36. If the mother was dead, the new priest included her among the beneficiaries of the mass and rescued her from purgatory.

Once He Starts, Luther Writes Rapidly

December 12, 1538

In these days, Luther was excited and anxious while in his mind he was thinking through the plan of his little book, A*gainst the Bishop of Magdeburg,* but when he began to write his quill moved rapidly. When asked about the swiftness of his pen he replied, "I bring forth what I conceive. I carefully consider all the arguments and every single word from every angle. The outline of a book like this requires a great deal of effort. This was the case with the writing on the abrogation of the mass. On the other hand, the papists and our other opponents simply burst forth and babble; they write whatever comes to mind."

What Fasting Was Like in the Monastery

March 20, 1539

On March 20, there was talk about the most sumptuous fasts of the papists—which were nothing less than fasts when the meals of bread and wine were without moderation. "Only truly afflicted consciences fasted in earnest," Martin Luther said. "I almost fasted myself to death, for again and again I went for three days without taking a drop of water or a morsel of food. I was very serious about it. I really crucified the Lord Christ. I wasn't simply an observer but helped to carry him and pierce [his hands and feet]. God forgive me for it, for I have confessed it openly! This is the truth: the most pious monk is the worst scoundrel. He denies that Christ is the mediator and high priest and turns him into a judge.

"I chose twenty-one saints and prayed to three every day when I celebrated mass; thus, I completed the number every week. I prayed especially to the Blessed Virgin, who with her womanly heart would compassionately appease her Son. Ah, if the article on justification hadn't fallen, the brotherhoods, pilgrimages, masses, invocation of saints, etc., would have found no place in the church. If it falls again (which may God prevent!) these idols will return."

Luther Does Not Wish to Live Much Longer

June 11, 1539

On June, 11 he [Martin Luther] went to Lichtenberg and had supper with the margrave's wife in the evening. She addressed him in a very friendly way, wished him a long life, and expressed the hope that he could live another forty years. He replied, "God forbid! Even if God were to offer me paradise in order that I might last forty more years in this life, I wouldn't want it. I'd rather hire a hangman to knock my head off. That's how bad the world is now. It's full of nothing but devils, so that one can't wish anything better than a blessed end and to get away. Nor do I bother with physicians. I won't embitter my life which may last a half year, but in God's name I'll eat whatever tastes good to me."

The Production of Books Seems Endless

Between July 1 and 10, 1539

He [Martin Luther] deplored the abundance of books and writers: "There will be a boundless flood of books, for any and everybody will be writing a book to feed his pride, while others will increase this evil in quest of gain. So, the Bible will be buried under a mass of literature about the Bible, and the text itself will be neglected, though the experts in the text are the best men in every discipline. . . . But today everybody hastens to consult writers.

"As a young man, I made myself familiar with the Bible; by reading it again and again I came to know my way about in it. Only then did I consult writers [of books about the Bible]. But finally, I had to put them out of my sight and wrestle with the Bible itself. It's better to see with one's own eyes than with another's. On this account, because of the bad example, I would wish that all my books were buried. Otherwise everybody will imitate me and try to become famous by writing, as if Christ had died for the sake of our fickle glory and not for the hallowing of his name."

Luther Expects No Pay for Teaching

August 24, 1540

When somebody asked the doctor [Martin Luther] about a biblical passage, the doctor's wife replied, joking, "Doctor, don't teach them for nothing! They are gathering many things together. Lauterbach[37] in fact has collected the most, and they were useful sayings."

The doctor interjected, "For thirty years I have taught and preached without charging anything. Why should I begin to sell something in my old age?"

Illness of Luther's Daughter Becomes Graver

September, 1542

When the illness of his daughter became graver he [Martin Luther] said, "I love her very much. But if it is thy will to take her, dear God, I shall be glad to know that she is with thee."

Afterward he said to his daughter, who was lying in bed, "Dear Magdalene, my little daughter, you would be glad to stay here with me, your father. Are you also glad to go to your Father in heaven?"

The sick girl replied, "Yes, dear Father, as God wills."

The father said, "You dear little girl!" [Then he turned away from her and said,] "The spirit indeed is willing, but the flesh is weak" [Matt 26:41]. I love her very much. If this flesh is so strong, what must the spirit be?" Among other things he then said, "In the last thousand years God has given to no bishop such great gifts as he has given to me (for one should boast of God's gifts). I'm angry with myself that I'm unable to rejoice from my heart and be thankful to God, though I do at times sing a little song and thank God. Whether we live or die, we are the Lord's [Rom 14:8]—in the genitive singular and not in the nominative plural."[38]

---

37. Anthony Lauterbach was one of those who took notes of the conversation at Luther's table.
38. In Latin *Domini sumus* can mean 'we are the Lord's' (where *Domini* is taken as genitive singular) or 'we are lords' (where *domini* is nominative plural). This was a favorite play on words by Luther.

Luther's Wife Comforted When Daughter Is Dying

September, 1542

When his wife wept loudly, Martin Luther comforted her: "Think where she's going. She'll get along all right. Flesh is flesh, spirit is spirit. Children don't argue. They believe what they're told. All things are simple for children. They die without anxiety, complaint, or fear of death, and they have little physical pain, as if they were falling asleep."

Description of the Death of Magdalene Luther

September 20, 1542

When his daughter was in the agony of death, he [Martin Luther] fell on his knees before the bed and, weeping bitterly, prayed that God might will to save her. Thus, she gave up the ghost in the arms of her father. Her mother was in the same room, but farther from the bed on account of her grief. It was after the ninth hour on the Wednesday after the Fifteenth Sunday after Trinity in the year 1542.

Luther's Daughter Magdalene Placed in Coffin

September, 1542

When his dead daughter was placed in a coffin, he [Martin Luther] said, "You dear little Lena! How well it has turned out for you!"

He looked at her and said, "Ah, dear child, to think that you must be raised up and will shine like the stars, yes, like the sun!"

The coffin would not hold her, and he said, "The little bed is too small for her."

[Before this,] when she died, he said, "I am joyful in spirit but I am sad according to the flesh. The flesh doesn't take kindly to this. The separation [caused by death] troubles me above measure. It's strange to know that she is surely at peace and that she is well off there, very well off, and yet to grieve so much!"

The Coffin Is Escorted from the Home

September, 1542

When people came to escort the funeral and friends spoke to him according to custom and expressed to him their sympathy, he [Martin Luther] said, "You should be pleased! I've sent a saint to heaven—yes, a living saint. Would that our death might be like this! Such a death I'd take this very hour."

The people said, "Yes, this is quite true. Yet everybody would like to hold on to what is his."

Martin Luther replied, "Flesh is flesh, and blood is blood. I'm happy that she's safely out of it. There is no sorrow except that of the flesh."

Again, turning to others, he said, "Do not be sorrowful. I have sent a saint to heaven. In fact, I have now sent two of them...."

The Love of Parents for Their Children

September, 1542

Often, he [Martin Luther] repeated the words given above: "I'd like to keep my dear daughter because I love her very much, if only our Lord God would let me. However, his will be done! Truly nothing better can happen to her, nothing better."

While she was still living he often said to her, "Dear daughter, you have another Father in heaven. You are going to go to him."

Philip Melanchthon said, "The feelings of parents are a likeness of divinity impressed upon the human character. If the love of God for the human race is as great as the love of parents for their children, then it is truly great and ardent."

A Girl Is Harder to Raise Than a Boy

September, 1542

When she was buried, he [Martin Luther] said, "There is a resurrection of the flesh."

When he returned home from the funeral he said, "My daughter is now fitted out in body and soul. We Christians now have nothing to complain about. We know that it should and must be so, for we are altogether certain about eternal life."

Thereupon he consoled himself by saying, "After all, one must make provision for the children, especially for the poor girls. We have no right to expect that somebody else will care for them. I don't worry about the boys because a boy supports himself, no matter what country he's in, as long as he's willing to work. But the poor girls must have a staff to lean on. A boy who is in school can gather alms,[39] and afterward he can become a fine man if he has a will to. A girl can't do this and can easily bring shame on herself. I'm very glad to give my daughter to our Lord God. According to the flesh I would gladly have had her, but since God has taken her away I am thankful to him."

Desire to Talk with Christ Before the End

September, 1542

Turning to Rorer' he [Martin Luther] said, "Be of good cheer, Master!"

He responded, "I have at some time heard a word from Your Reverence that has often comforted me, namely, 'I have prayed our Lord God that he may grant me a blessed end in order that I may depart from this life, and I'm sure he'll do it. Just before I die I'll speak with Christ, my Lord, even if it should be but a brief word.'"

The doctor said, "I'm afraid I'll go suddenly and silently, without being able to utter a single word."

Philip Melanchthon said, "Whether we live or die we are the Lord's [Rom 14:8]. Even if you should fall down the stairs or should suddenly expire while you are writing, it wouldn't matter. Let it be! The devil hates us but God protects and keeps us."

---

39. It had been customary in Luther's youth for students to beg for alms. This practice was forbidden where the Reformation took hold.

Luther's Last Observation Left in a Note

February 16, 1546

"Nobody can understand Vergil in his *Bucolics* and *Georgics*[40] unless he has first been a shepherd or a farmer for five years. "Nobody understands Cicero in his letters unless he has been engaged in public affairs of some consequence for twenty years. "Let nobody suppose that he has tasted the Holy Scriptures sufficiently unless he has ruled over the churches with the prophets for a hundred years. Therefore, there is something wonderful, first, about John the Baptist; second, about Christ; third, about the apostles. 'Lay not your hand on this divine Aeneid, but bow before it, adore its every trace.'

'We are beggars. That is true."

These were the last thoughts of Dr. Martin Luther on the day before he died.

---

40. Vergil was the greatest of the Latin poets (70–19 B.C.); his *Bucolics* are poems about the life of shepherds and his *Georgics* are poems about agriculture and farmers.

7

Miscellaneous Table Talks

Marriage Should Begin with Prayer

Between February and March, 1532

"Marriage consists of these things: the natural desire of sex, the bringing to life of offspring, and life together with mutual fidelity. Yet the devil can so rupture marriage that hate is never more bitter than here. This comes from our beginning everything without prayer and with presumption. A God-fearing young man who is about to be married should pray, 'Dear God, add thy blessing!' But this is not done. . . . What is our Lord God to do under the circumstances? It is implied that his name is false: Almighty, Creator, the Giver of all things. Accordingly, dear Master Veit,[1] do as I did. When I wished to take my Katy, I prayed to God earnestly. You ought to do this too. You have never yet prayed to God earnestly for a wife."

---

1. Veit Dietrich, the recorder of the early table talks, was contemplating marriage.

The Magistrate Needs God's Help

April, 1532

"The magistrate is a minister of God. By himself he cannot maintain civil discipline. He is like a net placed in the water, and our Lord God chases the fish into the net. He drives wrongdoers into the net so that they do not slip away. It would be impossible if there were no divine judgment which declares, 'Either you repent or you are punished.' Likewise [it is written], 'There is a God who judges on earth' [Ps 58:11]. Consequently, nobody who does not repent will escape from the punishment of the magistrate. Even if you get away from me, you will not run away from the hangman."

An Auditor Is Encouraged to Marry

Between April 7 and 15, 1532

"You can't be without a wife and remain without sin. After all, marriage is an ordinance and creation of God. Therefore, it is not Satan's idea when a man desires to marry an honorable girl, for Satan hates this kind of life. So, make the venture in the name of the Lord and on the strength of his blessing and institution!"

The Painfulness of Separation in Death

Between April 20 and May 16, 1532

"There is no sweeter union than that in a good marriage. Nor is there any death more bitter than that which separates a married couple. Only the death of children comes close to this; how much this hurts I have myself experienced."

Some Conjectures About the Future Life

Summer, 1532

"In the future life, we'll have enjoyment of every kind and the whole earth will be adorned with many trees and all things that are pleasant to look at. If we have our Lord God we'll have enough. We'll be children of God. I don't believe that we shall all be of the same stature, and there will be no marriage; otherwise everybody will want to be a woman or a man."

Dissembling Is Necessary to Ruling

Summer or Fall, 1532

"There must be law in the administration of the household and of the government, for sin should not be tolerated. But if sin is committed there should be forgiveness; otherwise everything is ruined. A husband ought to overlook many things in his wife and children, but he ought not give up the law. It is so in all stations of life. There is forgiveness of sins in all creatures. Not all the trees grow upright, not all the streams flow in a straight line, the soil is not the same everywhere, etc. The judgment is therefore right: he who does not know how to dissemble does not know how to rule. This is clemency.[2] One must be tolerant without giving up all restraints. As they say, 'Neither everything nor nothing.'"

Adoration and Service Related to Law and Gospel

Summer or Fall, 1533

"First of all, adoration is of two kinds, true and false. Second, true adoration is of two kinds. On the one hand, it is external, as in bending the knee, bowing, uncovering the head, etc. On the other hand, it is internal, as in acknowledging the benefits of God, giving thanks, believing, etc. To serve, however, is to do something. So, one adores with one's face turned toward the Lord, but when one serves [a neighbor] one's back is turned toward the Lord. Adoration [is related to] the gospel, and service [is related to] the law."

God Appears to Be Too Severe and Too Lenient

Summer or Fall, 1588

"Our Lord God is always in the wrong, no matter what he does. He condemned Adam for disobedience when he ate of the fruit of the

---

2. Greek: *epieikeia*, 'equity.'

tree.[3] Reason considers only the object of obedience, and so God is said to have gone too far. On the other hand, God freely forgives all sins, even the crucifixion of his Son, provided men believe, and this is also regarded as going too far. Who can bring these two into harmony—the greatest severity and the greatest liberty and indulgence (as it seems to reason)? Therefore, it is said, 'Become like children' [Matt 18:3]."

The World Is Like a Drunken Peasant

Fall, 1533

"The world is like a drunken peasant. If you lift him into the saddle on one side, he will fall off on the other side. One can't help him, no matter how one tries. He wants to be the devil's."

Children Are Examples of Guilelessness

April 5, 1533

I told him [Martin Luther] on April 5, 1533, that my daughter Anastasia, who was then five years old, often spoke with the greatest confidence about Christ, the angels, heavenly joys, etc. I once said to her, "Oh, if one could but believe such things!" and she asked with a certain childlike seriousness whether I didn't believe them.

He [Martin Luther] replied that there is a remarkable innocence in children, and therefore Christ has set them before us as our teachers; they know no sin of envy, avarice, unbelief, etc., and take an apple for a gold piece. Hence Peter wrote [1 Pet 2:2] that newborn babes long for nothing but [the pure spiritual milk], etc.

Humankind's Arrogance and Self-Assurance

Early November, 1531

"It's remarkable that people should be so arrogant and secure when there are so many, indeed countless, evidences around us to suggest that we ought to be humble. The hour of our death is uncertain. The

---

3. Cf. Gen 3:17.

grain on which we live is not in our hands. Neither the sun nor the air, on which our life depends, lies in our power, and we have no control over our sleeping and waking. I shall say nothing of spiritual things, such as the private and public sins which press upon us. Yet our hearts are hard as steel and pay no attention to such evidence."

God Is Friendlier to Us Than Katy to Her Child

Before December 14, 1531

"God must be much friendlier to me and speak to me in friendlier fashion than my Katy to little Martin. Neither Katy nor I could intentionally gouge out the eye or tear off the head of our child. Nor could God. God must have patience with us. He has given evidence of it, and therefore he sent his Son into our flesh in order that we may look to him for the best.

"I think Paul himself was hostile to God because he couldn't believe as he wished he could.

"When I reflect on the magnitude of God's mercy and majesty, I am myself horrified at how far God has humbled himself."

Moses and Luther at the Last Judgment

Before December 14, 1531

"I won't tolerate Moses because he is an enemy of Christ. If he appears with me before the judgment I'll turn him away in the name of the devil and say, 'Here stands Christ.'

"In the last judgment, Moses will look at me and say, 'You have known and understood me correctly,' and he will be favorably disposed to me."

The Gospel Is Preached Through Music

Before December 14, 1531

"What is law doesn't make progress, but what is gospel does. God has preached the gospel through music, too, as may be seen in Josquin,[4] all of whose compositions flow freely, gently, and cheerfully, are not forced or cramped by rules, and are like the song of the finch."

Abundance of God's Gifts Taken for Granted

December 28, 1531

On the day of the Innocents [Martin Luther said]. "If God were to withhold our necessities from us for a year, what a cry there would be throughout the world! But now that he lavishes them upon us we're all ungrateful, and there is no one who gives thanks."

Signs on Every Hand of the Last Day

January 1, 1532

"The last day is at hand. My calendar has run out. I know nothing more in my Scriptures. All the firmaments and the course of the heavens are slowing down and approaching the end. For a whole year, the Elbe has remained at the same level, and this, too, is a portent."

The Great Saints Were Also Great Sinners

Between January 8 and March 23, 1532

"Let David be a prominent example of divine mercy. He tore apart a lion, he choked a devil when he slew Goliath, and he enjoyed God's favor, but afterward he tripped over a couple of pig tails.[5] Shame on you! He was also a murderer and became haughty. I think he canceled out his achievements. He almost was the greatest of all.

"John the Baptist was the holiest, for he had Christ's testimony. Next was Moses, then David, Elijah, etc. I think Moses, Aaron, and his sister also canceled out the good they did. When God said, 'because both of you broke faith with me among the Israelites at the waters of Meribath-kadesh. . . . you shall not enter . . .' [Deut 32:51, 52], he would have died quickly if he hadn't taken hold of the forgiveness of sins."

---

4. Josquin de Prez (d. 1521), a church musician on the eve of the Reformation whose compositions were prized by Luther and often sung at his table.
5. I.e., over a woman (Bathsheba) Cf. 2 Sam 11:2–12, 25.

Death Is Caused by Satan, Not by God

Between January 8 and March 23, 1532

"The devil slays us all, for the Scripture states that he causes death and is the author of death [John 8:44]. Satan put God's Son to death."

The doctor's wife said, "Oh. no, my dear Doctor! I don't believe it!"

Then the doctor said, "Who would love our Lord God if he himself had a mind to kill us? He won't be a murderer because he commanded, 'You shall not kill' [Exod 20:13]. If our Lord God wanted to kill me, it wouldn't matter inasmuch as I can expect good neither in heaven nor on earth. Besides, snakes, adders, toads, wolves, bears, lions—they all kill. What am I to expect?

"Everything that God makes he creates for life. He created things that they might be, and he called into being things that didn't exist, as if they did [Rom 4:17]. This means that life belongs to God's purpose. But death has been introduced into the world through the devil's envy, and on this account the devil is called the author of death. For what else does Satan do than seduce from true religion, provoke sedition, cause wars, pestilence, etc., and bring about every evil?"

Christ's Power Is Hidden to the World

Between January 8 and March 23, 1532

"Christ governs his kingdom in a remarkable way. He hides himself so that none of his power may be seen, and yet he confounds kings and emperors. Not even the pope can resist this power. Full assurance about this is necessary. To be sure, I know that even Paul had weakness in his faith. Hence, those boasts of his: 'I am a servant of God, an apostle of Jesus Christ' [Titus 1:1]. When he was on the sea an angel appeared to him and consoled him, and when the brethren who were on their way to Rome met him he took courage. So, you see what the fellowship of the godly does. The Lord wishes them to stay together and comfort one another, for he knows that they will have adversaries."

Explanation of Why the Disciples Were Afraid

April 7, 1532

Then I asked the doctor about that fear of the disciples which the evangelist mentioned, "the doors of the house where the disciples had met were locked for fear of the Jews" [John 20:19], inasmuch as we don't read in the gospel that the Jews had at that time undertaken any action against them.

The doctor replied to this question, "The apostles had seen what had happened to their Lord Christ, and so they were afraid that the same thing might happen to them as had happened to their master. They were also fearful because they could hardly believe that he had risen from the dead, for they said on the way to Emmaus, 'We had hoped that he was the one to redeem Israel' [Luke 24:21], just as if it was all over."

Then I said, "But they didn't preach until the coming of the Holy Spirit."

He replied, "He was promised to them in today's Gospel, when Christ said to them, 'Receive the Holy Spirit' [John 20:22]. But it's written in Luke [24:49], 'Stay here in the city until you have been clothed with power from on high.' It's as if he would say, 'I'll place armor on you that will withstand every shot.'"

Story of the Devil Breaking Up a Marriage

Between April 7 and May 1, 1532

"When I was a boy the story was once told about Satan's inability to start a quarrel between a man and his wife who loved each other deeply. He achieved his purpose through an old woman, who placed a sharp knife under the pillow of each of them. Then she told each [about the knife under the other's pillow]. The man found the knife [under his wife's pillow] and killed his wife. Then Satan approached the old woman and held out a pair of shoes to her on a long stick. When she asked why he didn't come closer Satan replied, 'You're worse than I am, for you've done to the man and his wife what I couldn't do.'

"So, we see that the devil is always hostile to whatever our Lord God does."

Luther Overtaken by a Spell of Dizziness

May 1, 1532

When Licentiate Melchior was elected on the fourth day after Cantate Sunday, I was present at the election. There Dr. Martin [Luther] began to feel dizzy. The doctor's wife sent a girl to fetch me. I went at once and saw that he was better. Then Dr. Jonas and Philip also arrived. Dr. Martin said to Jonas, "Dr. Jonas, let's make an exchange. I'll take your stone, and you take my weak head." Then Master Philip said, "If the sicknesses of all men were exchanged, it would probably be as Herodotus said: every man would want to have his own sickness again, and no man would be willing to exchange it."

Severe Whipping Makes Children Resentful

Between May 20 and 27, 1532

"One shouldn't whip children too hard. My father once whipped me so severely that I ran away from him, and he was worried that he might not win me back again. I wouldn't like to strike my little Hans very much, lest he should become shy and hate me. I know nothing that would give me greater sorrow. God acts like this [for he says], 'I'll chastise you, my children, but through another—through Satan or the world—but if you cry out and run to me, I'll rescue you and raise you up again.' For God doesn't want us to hate him."

Each Age Has Its Own Peculiar Temptations

Between May 27 and 31, 1532

"Young fellows are tempted by girls, men who are thirty years old are tempted by gold, when they are forty years old they are tempted by honor and glory, and those who are sixty years old say to themselves, 'What a pious man I have become!'"

Pope Deprived of the Blessing of Offspring

Between May 27 and 31, 1532

"That God has hated the pope appears from this, that God has deprived him of the fruit of his body. We wouldn't have received the blessing [of children] if the Lord hadn't planted the desire in us. The ardor is in both [men and women], and children are engendered as a consequence. Even if a child is unattractive when it is born, we nevertheless love it."

We Must Often Try God's Patience

Between May 27 and 31, 1532

The doctor took his son on his lap, and the child befouled him. Thereupon he [Martin Luther] said, "How our Lord God has to put up with many a murmur and stink from us, worse than a mother must endure from her child!"

Infant Is Example of Trust in God

June 8 or 9, 1532

When his infant son Martin was being suckled at his mother's breast, the doctor said, "The pope, the bishops, Duke George, Ferdinand, and all the demons hate this child, yet the little child isn't afraid of all of them put together. He sucks with pleasure at those breasts, is cheerful, is unconcerned about all his enemies, and lets them rage as long as they wish. Christ said truly, 'Unless you become like children,'" etc. [Matt 18:3].

Men Cannot Get Along Without Women

Between June 12 and July 12, 1532

"Many good things may be perceived in a wife. First, there is the Lord's blessing, namely, offspring. Then there is community of property. These are some of the pre-eminently good things that can overwhelm a man.

"Imagine what it would be like without this sex. The home, cities, economic life, and government would virtually disappear. Men can't do without women. Even if it were possible for men to beget and bear children, they still couldn't do without women."

Marriage and Cohabitation Are God's Creation

Between June 12 and July 12, 1532

"When one looks back upon it, marriage isn't so bad as when one looks forward to it. We see that our mothers and our fathers were saints and that we have the divine commandment, 'Honor your father and your mother' [Exod 20:12]. When I look beside myself, I see my brothers and sisters and friends, and I find that there's nothing but godliness in marriage. To be sure, when I consider marriage, only the flesh seems to be there. Yet my father must have slept with my mother and made love to her, and they were nevertheless godly people. All the patriarchs and prophets did likewise. The longing of a man for a woman is God's creation—that is to say, when nature's sound, not when it's corrupted as it is among Italians and Turks."

Wine for Old People, Milk for Children

Between June 12 and July 12, 1532

Dr. Martin Luther [said], "Old people should be given wine. Young children should slake their thirst with milk. Before the age of eight years no child should be given wine to drink."

Protective Angels Destructive Demons

Between November 24 and December 8, 1532

"The angels are very close to us and protect us and other creatures of God at his command. To be able to protect us they have long arms, and so they can easily chase Satan away when he tries to harm us. They stand before the face of the Father, next to the sun, but without effort they swiftly come to our aid. The devils, too, are very near to us. Every moment they are plotting against our life and welfare, but the angels prevent them from harming us. Hence it is that they don't always harm us although they always want to harm us.

"There are many demons in the woods, water, swamps, and deserted places who may not injure people. Others are in dense clouds and cause storms, lightning, thunder, and hail and poison the air. Philosophers and physicians attribute these things to nature and I don't know what other causes," etc.

When Women Try to Run Everything

Between December 11, 1532 and January 2, 1533
When he [Martin Luther] was arguing with his wife he said, "You convince me of whatever you please. You have complete control. I concede to you the control of the household, provided my rights are preserved. Female government has never done any good. God made Adam master over all creatures, to rule over all living things, but when Eve persuaded him that he was lord even over God she spoiled everything.[6] We have you women to thank for that! With tricks and cunning women deceive men, as I, too, have experienced."

A Dog Suggests a Topic for Comment

Between December 11, 1532 and January 2, 1533
Dr. Martin Luther played with his dog and said, "The dog is a very faithful animal and is held in high esteem if he isn't too ordinary. Our Lord God has made the best gifts most common. The pre-eminent gift given to all living things is the eye. Small birds have very bright eyes, like little stars, and can see a fly a room-length away. But we don't acknowledge such everyday gifts. We are stupid clods. In the future life we'll see them, however; there we ourselves will make birds with pretty, shining eyes."

Adam Would Be Astonished by Our Life

Between December 11, 1532 and January 2, 1533
"If Adam were to return and see our life, food, drink, dress, etc., oh, how he would wonder about it! He would say, 'I have never

---

6. Cf. Gen 1:28; 3:1–7.

been in this world. Perhaps some other Adam has been in this world first.' [So, he would think] because he drank water, ate of the fruit of the trees, put up a hut with four gable walls, had no knife and no iron, and put on a covering made of hides. Now, however, there are immense expenditures for food and drink and we have palatial houses and highly ornamented garments. The ancients lived frugally. It was as Boaz said, 'Dip your bread in vinegar. Strengthen your heart with bread.' The lands were populous, as we see in the book of Joshua, and therefore the multitude of people produced thrift."

The Last Will of a Man of the World

Between January 2 and 26, 1533
"It's a remarkable and very offensive thing that the world is constantly degenerating more and more, though the gospel has been preached often. Everybody interprets the spiritual liberty of Christ as if it were carnal pleasure. In external matters, therefore, the kingdom of Satan and the kingdom of the pope are best for the world, for the world wishes to be governed by laws, the lies of superstition, and tyranny and is only made worse by the doctrine of grace because it doesn't believe that there is any future life after this one. This was demonstrated by the man who, when he was dying, set down his written will and testament in a letter in which nothing was read but these words: 'As long as I could I robbed. Rob as long as you can!'"

A Suggestion for Students on Reading

Between January 2 and 26, 1533
"A student who doesn't want his work to go for nothing ought to read and reread some good author until the author becomes part, as it were, of his flesh and blood. Scattered reading confuses more than it teaches. Many books, even good ones, have the same effect on the student. So, he is like the man who dwells everywhere and therefore dwells nowhere. Just as in human society we don't enjoy the fellowship of every friend every day, but only of a few chosen ones, so we ought to do in our studies."

Christians and Heathen Face Death

May 15, 1532

"Christians could easily suffer death if they didn't know that God's wrath is connected with it. This circumstance makes death a bitter thing for us. The heathen, on the contrary, die confidently; they don't see God's wrath but think death is the end of man. They say, 'It doesn't amount to anything but a bad moment.' But Cicero put it excellently, 'Afterward we'll be nothing or we'll be altogether blessed.' It's as if he would say, 'Nothing bad can happen to us as a consequence of death.'"

Every Seventh Year Brings a Change

June 5, 1532

"My Hans is about to enter upon his seventh year, which is always climacteric, that is, a time of change. People always change every seventh year. The first period of seven years is childhood, and at the second change—say, in the fourteenth year—boys begin to look out into the world; this is the time of boyhood, when the foundations are laid in the arts. At the age of twenty-one youths desire marriage, in the twenty-eighth year young men are householders and heads of families, while at the age of thirty-five men have civil and ecclesiastical positions. This continues to the age of forty-two, when we are kings. Soon after this, men begin to lose their sense. So, every seventh year always brings to man some new condition and way of life. This has happened to me, and it happens to everybody."

Much Adjustment Required in Marriage

June, 1532

"Man has strange thoughts the first year of marriage. When sitting at table he thinks, 'Before I was alone; now there are two.' Or in bed, when he wakes up, he sees a pair of pigtails lying beside him which he hadn't seen there before. On the other hand, wives bring to their husbands, no matter how busy they may be, a multitude of trivial matters. So my Katy used to sit next to me at first while I was studying hard and would spin and ask, 'Doctor, is the grandmaster the margrave's brother?'"

Fishing and Eating Fish with Pleasure

Fall, 1533

Dr. Luther went out with his wife into the garden to fish in the pond and on the bank of the river. There they caught pike, loach, trout, blacktail, carp. Some of them we ate at the table with great delight and thanksgiving. The doctor said, "Katy, you are more pleased over these few fish than many a nobleman when he fishes in several large ponds and catches thousands of fish. Alas, greed and ambition prevent us from enjoying things. Many a skinflint sits in the midst of the greatest luxuries and yet can't enjoy them with pleasure. It's said that the ungodly won't see the glory of God; in fact, they can't even recognize present gifts because God overwhelms us so much with them. If they were rare, we might esteem them more highly. But we can't reflect on the pleasure which the creatures give.

"See how well a little fish multiplies, for one produces probably a thousand! It happens this way, that the male strikes with his tail, deposits sperm in the water, and from it the female conceives. Consider the birds, how chastely their reproduction takes place! The rooster pecks the hen's head, the hen lays a little egg nicely in the nest, sits on it, and soon the young chick peeps out. Look how the little chick is hidden in the egg! If we had never seen such an egg and one were brought from Shangrila, we'd all be startled and amazed. And all the philosophers couldn't offer an explanation for these creatures. Only Moses gives an explanation: 'God said, and it was so' [Gen 1:9]. He commanded, and they were made. 'Be fruitful and multiply' [Gen 1:22]. And so it goes on."

Revival of Music and Gymnastics Proposed

October 27, 1536

"Excellent was the arrangement of the ancients that required men to exercise, lest they fall into debauchery, drunkenness, and gambling. I especially admire these two noble exercises, music and gymnastics. The first of these pertains to the spirit and serves to drive away care, while the second pertains to the body and practices the limbs by jumping and wrestling. The most important reason [for engaging in these exercises] is that we don't fall into other habits of drink, lust, and gambling such as we now, alas, see at the courts and in the cities. There one hears nothing but 'Here's to you! Drink it down!' Then one plays for a hundred florins. This is what happens when noble exercises are despised."

Increased Cost of Living in Wittenberg

Between October 27 and December 4, 1536
Master Philip spoke about the high cost of living in this town and said that a student requires twice as much money now as ten years ago. Dr. Martin Luther replied, "We see by experience. When farmers hear the pastors complaining about a shortage of food, they say, 'Oho, but they were able to make out before!' To this I have often responded, 'Yes, when one could buy fifteen eggs for four pieces of copper and a bushel of rye for two pieces of silver, they were able to manage. But now that everything sells for three times as much, the cost of living has tripled while the pay is still the same.' Truly the farmer has now learned arithmetic; he knows how to double his cubic numbers."

Why Does the First Drink Taste Best?

Between October 27 and December 4, 1536
"How is it that the first drink from a tankard tastes best? Perhaps it's on account of sin, because our flesh and our lips are sinful."

Troubles Outside of Marriage and Inside

Between December 16 and 18, 1536
"He who takes a wife is not idle, for marriage keeps him busy. To remain continent in celibacy confronts one with temptations that are not trivial, as the experienced know. On the other hand, the annoy-

ances of married life are [almost] unbearable to men. Accordingly, Socrates is reported to have given a good answer to a man who was contemplating marriage: Whatever you may do, you'll regret it. In paradise, where there was no such ardor and raging passion, marriage must have been very pleasant. Flesh and blood were different then. But we have become so infected with original sin that there's no kind of life which, once undertaken, isn't a matter of regret at times. This is the fault of our original sin, which has defiled and deformed all human nature. It seems to me that it is the pleasantest kind of life to have a moderate household, to live with an obedient wife, and to be content with little." He [Martin Luther] looked up to heaven [and sighed], "Dear God, how art thou to arrange things so as to please us?"

Two Kinds of Adultery in the Sight of God

Between December 16 and 18, 1536

In God's sight adultery is of two kinds. The first is Matthew 5 [:27–28], which nobody escapes. [The second is] John 8 [:3–11] and is horrible. Yet it is praised, so that a prominent man said to Luther, "I didn't think adultery was such a great sin." But it is a sin against God, against the Holy Spirit, against civil authority, against domestic life....

Changed Attitude Toward Play and Games

Between January 14 and 31, 1537

"Games with cards and dice are common, for our age has invented many games. Surely there has been a reaction. In my youth, all games were prohibited; makers of cards and musicians at dances weren't admitted to the sacraments, and people were required to make confession of their gaming, dancing, and jousting. Today these things are the vogue, and they are defended as exercises for the mind."

Marriage Followed by Love or Regret

Between January 14 and 31, 1537
"It's the greatest blessing of God when love continues to flower in marriage. The first love is ardent, an intoxicated love which dazzles us and leads us on. When the intoxication has been slept off, the connubial love of the godly is genuine, while the ungodly have regrets."

Things Might Have Been Different

Between January 14 and 31, 1537
"Oh, how wonderful, beyond anything imaginable, our condition would have been if Adam hadn't fallen! Everything would have turned out according to God's command and Word. Adam would have said to Eve, 'God said that I am male and you are female.' They wouldn't have had to milk a cow or whistle to a dog. Everything would have happened according to God's Word. But now we do everything by habit without giving thanks."

Modern Instruments of War Deplored

March 19, 1537
Afterward he [Martin Luther] spoke of firearms and cannons, those most inhuman devices which smash walls and rocks and slay men in battle. "I think these things were invented by Satan himself, for they can't be defended against with [ordinary] weapons and fists. All human strength vanishes when confronted with firearms. A man is dead before he sees what's coming. If Adam had seen such devices as his descendants have constructed to fight one another, he would have died of grief."

Interpretation of the Inheritance of Widows

Between June 18 and July 28, 1537
"The greatest right is the greatest wrong. Consequently, there is need of a good interpreter, as in the case of that law in the Saxon code, 'After a man dies his widow should be given a stool and a coat.'

Many a woman has worked in her household for thirty or forty years; if she ought to get what is according to the letter of the law, should it be worth only a penny? After all, servants must be paid better than this. Even an unknown beggar who stops at the door is given this much at a time. The word 'stool' must therefore be interpreted to mean house and home, and the word 'coat' should mean the sustenance by means of which she may maintain herself in her old age. This is the intention of that law, yet here and there some men wish to observe it literally and kick widows out as they would dogs."

Acknowledging God's Gifts in the Cherry Season

Between June 18 and July 28, 1537

Dr. Justus Jonas praised the glorious blessing which God grants in fruit. "I have a branch with cherries on it hanging over my table," he said, "in order that when I look at it I may learn the article about divine creation."

Dr. Martin Luther responded, "Why don't you learn it daily by looking at your children, the fruit of your body? They're there every day, and surely they amount to much more than all the fruit of the trees! There you may see the providence of God, who created them from nothing. In half a year he gave them body, life, and limb, and he will also sustain them. Yet we overlook them, as if those gifts of God made us blind and greedy, as it usually happens that men become worse and more greedy when they have offspring; they don't realize that every child is apportioned his lot according to the saying, 'The more children the more luck.' Dear God, how great are the ignorance and the wickedness of man, who doesn't think about the best gifts of God but does just the opposite."

The Use and Abuse of Music

Between August 81 and October 11, 1537

He [Martin Luther] asked somebody if he was a musician. When the latter replied that he knew nothing about music, he [Martin Luther] responded, "Oh, the art is a noble commodity. One shouldn't use it for pay, for purse or coffer. The art is easy to practice, is esteemed everywhere, benefits all people, and nevertheless preserves its own integrity. Yet nobody wants to learn or love it."

A Story Serves as Parable of the World

Between November 1 and December 21, 1537

"A man once rented an ass to ride on. The owner of the ass went on foot next to the rider. When it got too hot for the rider on the ass, he asked the owner to ride so that he might walk in the shade alongside. The owner of the ass was unwilling to do this because he had rented the ass to him for riding and not the ass's shadow. For the latter, he would have to pay extra.

"This is a picture of the world, which doesn't give anything for nothing, not even a shadow."

Consolation for a Depressed Friend

March 29, 1538

Thereupon Dr. Weller arrived very troubled and depressed. Luther comforted him and told him to give his heart to the Lord and seek fellowship with men. Luther asked whether he was angry with God or with Luther or with himself.

Weller replied, "I confess that I am murmuring against God." To this Luther said, "God will give up nothing. I, too, often honor God in this way. When I should procure good incense for him I bring him the stinking pitch and fetid dung of murmuring and impatience. If we didn't have the article concerning the forgiveness of sins (which God has promised surely to keep) we'd be in a bad way."

Weller said, "The devil is a master at taking hold of us where it hurts most."

Luther: "Yes, he doesn't learn this from us. He is quite agile. If he hasn't exempted the patriarchs, the prophets, and the prince of prophets, Christ, he will not spare us. He can make the oddest syllogisms: 'You have sinned. God is angry with sinners. Therefore despair!' Accordingly, we must proceed from the law to the gospel and grasp the article concerning the forgiveness of sins. You are not the only one, dear brother, who suffers from such anguish. Peter admonishes us not to be surprised when the same experience of suffering is required of the brotherhood. Moses, David, and Isaiah suffered much and often. What kind of trials do you suppose David was going through when he composed the psalm, 'O Lord, do not rebuke me in your anger' [Ps 6:1]? He would rather have died by the sword than to have experienced these horrible feelings against God and of God against him. I believe that confessors have to endure more than martyrs, for day after day they see idolatries, offenses, and sins, the prosperity and security of the godless, and on the other hand the anxieties of the godly who are accounted as sheep for the slaughter."[7]

Continuation of the Consolation

March 29, 1538

Thereupon he entreated Weller to cultivate the company of men when he is afflicted with such melancholy and not live alone. "'Woe to one who is alone,' the preacher says [Eccles 4:10]. When I'm morose I flee above all from solitude. Christ was himself tempted by Satan when our Lord was alone in the wilderness.[8] On the other hand, the wilderness of John the Baptist[9] was inhabited . . . he was among men. In short, spiritual anguish exceeds bodily suffering by far. The anguish of Judas—'you have betrayed innocent blood'—became for him the most awful death.

"This is especially so when the devil turns the gospel into law. The teachings of law and gospel are altogether necessary, but they must be distinguished even when they are conjoined, otherwise men will despair or become presumptuous. Consequently, Moses describes these teachings well when he speaks of an upper and lower millstone.[10] The upper millstone rumbles and pounds. This is the law. It's very well set up by God so that it grinds. On the other hand, the lower millstone is quiet, and this is the gospel. Our Lord God has sus-

---

7. Cf. Ps 44:22.
8. Cf. Matt 4:1–11.
9. Cf. Matt 3:1.
10. Cf. Deut 24:6.

pended the upper millstone in such a way that the grain is crushed and ground only on the lower stone.

"This is my only and my best advice: Don't remain alone when you are assailed! Flee solitude! Do as that monk did who, when he felt tempted in his cell, said, 'I won't stay here; I'll run out of the cell to my brethren.' So, it's reported of Paul in the book of Acts [27:33; 28:15] that he suffered for fourteen days from severe hunger and from shipwreck and afterward was received by his brethren and took courage. This is what I do too. I'd rather go to my swineherd John, or even to the pigs themselves, than remain alone."

How to Deal with Specters and Poltergeists

April 5, 1538

On April 5, a pastor came from the church in Süptitz, near Torgau, to complain of apparitions and disturbances caused by Satan. He said that Satan disturbed his peace with nocturnal tumults and the smashing of all the utensils in his house. Satan hurled pots and dishes close to his head, so that they broke in pieces, and Satan annoyed him by laughing out loud, although he saw nothing of him. For a whole year, the pastor said, he had endured these and many other trials, so that his wife and children wished to leave [the house].

Luther responded, "Dear Brother, be strong in the Lord and firm in your faith! Don't give in to that robber! Suffer the outward things and the minor damage that comes from the breaking of pots, for it can't harm you in body and soul, as you have found, for the angel of the Lord is with you. Let Satan play with the pots. Meanwhile pray to God with your wife and children and say, 'Be off, Satan! I'm lord in this house, not you. By divine authority I'm head of this household, and I have a call from heaven to be pastor of this church. I have testimony from heaven and earth, and this is what I rely on. You enter this house as a thief and robber. You are a murderer and a scoundrel. Why don't you stay in heaven? Who invited you to come here?' In this way, you should sing him his litany and his legend and let him play as long as he pleases.

"I was often pestered [by the devil] when I was imprisoned in my

Patmos, high up in the fortress in the kingdom of the birds.[11] I resisted him in faith and confronted him with this verse: God, who created man, is mine, and all things are under his feet.[12] If you have any power over him, try it!"

Then he told a story about a woman in Magdeburg who, when Satan disturbed her, drove him away by breaking wind. "This example is not always to be followed and is dangerous," Luther said, "because Satan, who is the spirit and author of presumption, is not easily mocked and put to flight. Reliance on such an example can prove that it's not at all appropriate for somebody else. So, it once happened that a horned specter of Satan lost his horn when a godly man boasted of his baptism, but when another man foolishly tried to imitate this example, he was killed by Satan."

Roman Comedies Made Youth Marry

May 29, 1538

"The comedies which the Romans produced please me most. It was their principal purpose to incite young people to marry, for political activity can't exist without marriage. On this account those ingenious people enticed the young people to marry as best they could by means of comedies as well as pictures. For whoring and celibacy are pests to the state."

What Will Occupy Us in Eternal Life

June 27, 1538

Then they spoke about eternal life and the joy that will exist then. "I often think about it [said Luther] but I can't imagine what it's like, can't understand how we'll spend our time inasmuch as there will be no change, no work, no food and drink, and nothing to occupy us there. But I think we'll have enough to do with God. Accordingly, Philip put it well when he said, 'Lord, show us the Father, and we will be satisfied' [John 14:8]. This will be our very dear preoccupation."

---

11. Luther referred to the Wartburg, the castle to which he was taken for his protection after the Diet of Worms in 1521, as his Patmos and as the kingdom of the birds.
12. Cf. Ps 8:6.

Death Comes to All After an Interval

August 1, 1538

"Astonishing is the stupidity of a man who fears death. Death is common to all men, and nobody can escape it. Cicero was able to comfort himself very well as a heathen in the first book of the Tusculans. How much more ought Christians do this, for they have Christ, the destroyer of death, and have [eternal] life and the resurrection. Even if we'd like to live longer, it's a brief interval at best. It's like many of you traveling to Düben; some of you will arrive there about the fourth hour and others about the seventh or eighth hour, but all of you will have to put up there for the night. So, Adam has preceded us by only a few hours; he has hardly had more than one night's rest more than us."

Luther Praises the Hospitals in Italy

August 1, 1538

Then Luther spoke about the hospital care of the Italians, how well provided their hospitals are: "They are splendidly built, the best food and drink are at hand, the attendants are very diligent, the physicians are learned, the beds and coverings are very clean, and the bedsteads are painted. As soon as a sick man is brought in, all his clothes are taken off in the presence of a notary and are faithfully kept for him. He is then dressed in a white smock and laid in a handsomely painted bed with clean sheets. Two physicians are fetched at once. Attendants come with food and drink, served in immaculate glass vessels; these are not touched with as much as a finger but are brought on a tray. Honorable matrons, who are completely veiled, come in, minister to the poor for several days without identifying themselves, and then go back to their homes.

"I have myself seen in Florence with what care the hospitals make provision [for the sick]. This is true also of foundling homes in which children are excellently kept, fed, and brought up; they are all dressed alike in the same color and are looked after in a paternal way."

We Do Not Know About the Future Life

August 7, 1538

On August 7, he [Martin Luther] said, "I was so gravely ill with this sickness that I committed my life to God's keeping. Nevertheless, during this time of my illness many things occurred to me. Oh, how I pondered over what eternal life is like and what its joys may be! Although I'm sure that it has been given to us by Christ and that it is ours even now because we have faith, it won't be made known to us until hereafter. It isn't given to us here to know what that creation of the next world is like, for we can't fathom this first creation of the world and its creatures.

"If I'd been with God before the creation of this world, I wouldn't have been able to give him this advice, that he ought to make such a large spherical device out of nothing and attach to it a brooch, the sun, which in its swift course illuminates the whole earth, nor that he ought to fashion man and woman as he did. All this God did for us without our counsel and design. So, we must accord him the honor of providing a future life and a new creation and let him remain the Creator."

The Quarreling and Reconciliation of Children

August 17, 1538

On August 17, he [Martin Luther] listened to the quarreling and fighting among his children and afterward watched them as they were again reconciled. Then he said, "Dear God, how pleased you must be with the life and play of such children! Yes, all their sins are nothing else than forgiveness of sins."

Why God Places Christians in the World

August 31, 1538

"God placed his church in the midst of the world, among countless external activities and callings, not in order that Christians should become monks but so that they may live in fellowship and that our works and the exercises of our faith may become known among men. For human society, as Aristotle said, is not an end in itself but a means [to an end]; and the ultimate end is to teach one another about God. ..."

Antinomian Leaders Are Called Hypocrites

October 11, 1538

"I think well of men who are open, who make a thing clear in word and gesture, and who are not liars and hypocrites like John Agricola and Jacob Schenk, who do everything in a friendly and yet deceitful way. The term 'hypocrite' is a very strong and emphatic designation, and Christ also employed it.[13] One couldn't rebuke a person more sharply than by calling him a hypocrite, that is, the worst possible pest."

Some Observations About Life in Heaven

December 6, 1538

On the same day, Luther spoke admirably about the future eternal life and its unspeakable joy: "Human reason can't grasp it by speculation. With our thoughts, we can't get beyond the visible and physical. No man's heart comprehends eternity. One might suppose that according to the saying, 'Even pleasure becomes burdensome,' one would get tired of eternity. What pleasure is like in eternity we can't imagine. Isaiah said, 'But be glad and rejoice forever in what I am creating' [Isa 65:18]."

Meditation at Table on Christmas Day

December 25, 1538

This evening he [Martin Luther] was very joyful. His conversation, his singing, and his thoughts were about the incarnation of Christ, our Savior. Amid his sighs he said, "Ah, what wretched people we are! To think that we are so cold and slothful in our attitude toward this great joy which, after all, happened for us, this great benefaction which is far, far superior to all other works of creation!

---

13. Cf. Luke 6:42.

And yet how hard it is for us to believe, though the good news was preached and sung for us by angels, who are heavenly theologians and have rejoiced in our behalf! Their song is the most glorious. It contains the whole Christian faith. For the *gloria in excelsis*[14] is supreme worship. They wish us such worship and they bring it to us in Christ.

"Ever since the fall of Adam the world knows neither God nor his creation. It lives altogether outside of the glory of God. Oh, what thoughts man might have had about the fact that God is in all creatures, and so might have reflected on the power and the wisdom of God in even the smallest flowers! Of a truth, who can imagine how God creates, out of the parched soil, such a variety of flowers, such pretty colors, such sweet vernal grass, beyond anything that a painter or apothecary[15] could make! Yet God can bring out of the ground such colors as green, yellow, red, blue, brown. Adam and those around him would have been elevated by all this to the praise of God, and they would have made use of all created things with thanksgiving. Now we enjoy all this to overflowing, yet without understanding, like cattle or other beasts trampling the most beautiful blossoms and lilies underfoot.

"For this reason, the angels here [in the Christmas story] recall fallen men to faith and love, that is, to glory toward God and peace on earth."

Children Are Ingenuous at Their Play

February 26, 1539

On February 26 Master Spalatin and the pastor of Zwickau, Master Leonard, came to supper [in Luther's house]. He [Martin Luther] had some pleasant banter with his little son Martin, who wished to defend his doll with zeal and honor and to dress her and love her. Then he said, "Such was our disposition in paradise—simple, upright, without malice. There must have been real earnestness there, just as this boy speaks about God piously and with supreme trust and just as he is sure

---

14. Latin: 'Glory to God in the highest' (Luke 2:14).
15. In the sixteenth century paints were prepared and sold by apothecaries.

of God. Such natural playing is best in children, who are the dearest jesters. The affected play of old fools lacks such grace. Therefore, little children are the finest mockingbirds and talk naturally and honestly. ..."

The Simplicity of Faith in Children

February 26, 1539

Afterward, watching his son, he [Martin Luther] praised the boy's ingenuousness and innocence: "Children are better informed in the faith [than adults], for they believe very simply and without any question in a gracious God and eternal life. Oh, how good it is for children to die while they're young. To be sure, it would cause me great grief because part of my body and part of their mother's flesh and blood would die. Such natural feelings don't cease in godly parents, no matter how hardened and calloused they think they are, for feelings like these are a work of divine creation.

"Children live altogether in faith, without reason. It's as Ambrose said, 'There is lack of reason but not of faith.'"

The Pope as Antichrist and the Devil Incarnate

April 11, 1539

"I believe the pope is the masked and incarnate devil because he is the Antichrist. As Christ is God incarnate, so the Antichrist is the devil incarnate. The words are really spoken of the pope when it's said that he's a mixed god, an earthly god, that is, a god of the earth. Here god is understood as god of this world. Why does he call himself an earthly god, as if the one, almighty God weren't also on the earth?

"The kingdom of the pope really signifies the terrible wrath of God, namely, the abomination of desolation standing in the holy place.[16] Therefore Christ says that he who reads this should mark it well. To be sure, it's very exasperating that after Christ's revelation a man should lift himself up above God in the church. If this had happened among the heathen before the revelation of Christ it wouldn't

---

16. Cf. Matt 24:15; Dan 12:11.

have been very remarkable. That's why we have been so diligently warned about this deadly pestilence by Daniel, Christ, Paul, Peter, and others. In spite of this, we Christians were so stupid that we asked for all the pope's commands.

"We allowed ourselves to be persuaded that, under the pretext of the patrimony of Peter,[17] he is the lord over the whole world, although neither Christ nor Peter bequeathed any kind of dominion on earth."

Good Weather and Promise of Crops

April 25, 1539

When fruitful weather set in, he [Martin Luther] said with a sigh, "Ah, praise God, this is wonderful weather! God is merciful and grants it to us without our deserving it. Would that we might also become more godly! If this happened we'd have paradise and heaven right here. All pains and troubles would be ended. Caterpillars, ants, and all sorts of worms would no longer harm our fruit, but everything would grow green and ripen in a delightful way.

However, the punishment of original sin goes out into the whole world and falls on all creatures. . . ."

Pleasures of a May Day in Late April

April 28, 1539

Afterward he gave thought to the pleasant weather in the month of May, whose blooms are a parable of the resurrection of the dead. "How pleasant the trees are! How delightfully green everything's beginning to be! It's like a charming day in May. I don't recall one like it. If it continues this way it will be a very fruitful year and the world will be crammed full. Ah, would that we could trust God! If God can take such delight in our earthly sojourn, what must it be like in the life to come?"

---

17. The alleged hereditary estates of St. Peter were the lands in Italy which the popes possessed. These were developed and added to especially by Pope Gregory I (590–604).

God Is More Generous Than We Expect

Between May 6 and 16, 1540

"Our Lord God always gives more than we ask for. If we ask properly for a piece of bread he gives us a whole acre. I prayed God to let my Katy live, and he gives her a good year in addition. But I think a really bad time will follow because we're too wicked and are introducing heresies among ourselves."

What Was God Doing Before the Creation?

Between May 21 and June 11, 1540

Severus said, "The scholastics even disputed about the question of where God was before the creation of the world. I heard Camers reply in Vienna that God was in himself."

The doctor [Martin Luther] said, "Yes, Augustine mentioned this. But once, when he was asked, he said, 'God was making hell for those who are inquisitive.'" Then he added, "Where is God now, after the creation?"

Why God Sometimes Winks at Wrong

June 11, 1540

The doctor's wife said, "If it were in my hands I would really take vengeance on my adversaries. Why does God spare them so?" The doctor replied, "If God were to do everything with his might, where would that leave his wisdom and his goodness? Accordingly, he overlooks many things so that his wisdom and goodness may become known in our weakness. It will turn out well."

What It Means to Be Delivered to Satan

Between June 11 and 19, 1540

Major said, "My dear doctors, I don't understand this passage [where Paul speaks of certain persons who had made a shipwreck of their faith and said he delivered them to Satan that they may learn not to blaspheme, 1 Tim 1:19, 20]. Explain it for me."

The doctor [Martin Luther] then said, "At the time of the apostles' miracles still occurred often. Accordingly, if they wished to punish somebody they delivered his body to the devil to be tormented. The body of such a person was possessed and harassed for a while by the devil. Thereupon the church prayed and the possessed person was set free, as we see in the history of the church. So, Nebuchadnezzar was punished for seven years and without doubt was afterward saved." [18]

Pomeranus observed: "One must take the historical context into account."

Then Major asked, "But if they died under this harassment, would they be damned?"

The doctor replied, "This was their penance to be tormented so. Accordingly, their soul would be saved."

Marriage of a Young Man and an Old Woman

Between September 2 and 17, 1540

[Somebody asked] whether a marriage between a young man and an old woman would be proper when there was no hope of offspring. The doctor [Martin Luther] replied, "Yes, indeed! Of the four reasons I gave in my Genesis the fourth is that such a marriage should be approved for the sake of honoring marriage. However, I'd prefer if at the wedding the words, 'Be fruitful and multiply,' were omitted. Yet I don't like to make ceremonies and regulations, for once one starts there's no end to it any more. One follows another, as in the papacy."

We Are Not Satisfied with God's Gifts

Between September 2 and 17, 1540

"How rich a God our God is! He gives enough, but we don't notice it. He gave the whole world to Adam, but this was nothing in Adam's eyes; he was concerned about the one tree and had to ask why God had forbidden him to eat of it. That's the way it is today too. God has given us enough to learn in his revealed Word, but we let this go and

---

18. Cf. Dan 4:28–37.

look for his hidden will without being able to find it. It serves us right if we are crushed as a consequence."

Forcing or Forbidding Children to Marry Is Wrong

Summer or Fall, 1542

"Secret marriages ought not to be considered valid at all, although our lawyers wish to recognize them as such. However, parents ought not urge their children to marry persons for whom they, the children, have no liking. On the other hand, parents ought to give their children permission to marry when they are of marriageable age, and they should not refuse them permission to take the sons or daughters of respectable people in marriage if the young people are attracted to each other.

"We once united a couple here against the will of the parents. The bridegroom was an honorable and well-to-do fellow; the bride was poor and would have been glad to have him but her father did not wish it, for he said he wanted her in the house. I replied, 'There are plenty of maidservants here; hire one for yourself!' And with that I united them in marriage."

Progress of the Gospel Is a Sign of the End

Summer or Fall, 1542

"I think the last day is not far away. My reason is that a last great effort is now being made to advance the gospel. It's like a candle. Just before it burns out it makes a last great spurt, as if it would continue to burn for a long time, and then it goes out. So, it now appears as if the gospel is going to spread far and wide, but I'm afraid that it will be extinguished in a jiffy and that the day of judgment will follow. That's how it is with a sick person too. When he's about to die he generally seems to be very alert, as if he might recover, and then in a jiffy he's gone."

Marriage Requires More Than Fleeting Feeling

Winter of 1542–1543

"After Lucas, the artist, had taken a wife and the wedding was over, he always desired to be next to his bride. He had a good friend who said to him, 'Friend, don't do that. Before a half year is gone you will have had enough of that. There won't be a maid in your house whom you won't prefer to your wife.' And so it is. We hate the things that are present and we love those that are absent. As Ovid wrote, 'What we may have [does not please us]; it's what we may not have that excites our passion.' This is the weakness of our nature. Then the devil comes and introduces hatred, suspicion, and concupiscence on both sides, and these cause desertion. It's easy enough to get a wife, but to love her with constancy is difficult. A man who can do this has reason to thank our Lord God for it.

"Accordingly, if a man intends to take a wife, let him be serious about it and pray to God, 'Dear Lord God, if it be thy divine will that I continue to live without a wife, help me to do so. If not, bestow upon me a good, pious girl with whom I may spend all my life, whom I hold dear, and who loves me.' There's more to it than a union of the flesh. There must be harmony with respect to patterns of life and ways of thinking. The bonds of matrimony alone won't do it."

Schools Are the Preservers of the Church

Winter of 1542–1543

"When schools flourish, things go well and the church is secure. Let us make more doctors and masters. The youth is the church's nursery and fountainhead. When we are dead, where are others [to take our place] if there are no schools? God has preserved the church through schools. They are the preservers of the church. Schools don't have a beautiful appearance, and yet they are very useful. Little boys have learned at least the Lord's Prayer and the Creed in the schools, and the church has been remarkably preserved through such small schools."

Index

absolution, 64, 72, 86
adoration, 73, 157
adultery, 7, 52, 61, 171
allegory, 56
alms, 31, 153
Anabaptists, 18, 31, 35n15, 72n3, 79
angels, 25, 52, 53, 55, 62, 65, 80, 118, 120, 131, 132, 158, 161, 165–66, 176, 181
antichrist, 182
Apostles' Creed, 23, 27, 51, 57n9, 93, 120, 129, 140, 188
Aquinas, Thomas, 71n1
Aristotle, 22, 117, 180
Arius, 104
Augsburg, 25n23, 81, 144–45, 147
Augustine, 28, 81, 89–90, 97, 104–5, 109, 111, 113, 116, 146, 184
authorship of Genesis, 64

baptism: infant, 73, 75–76, 78–79, 81–82, 137
begging, 5n2

Bernard of Clairvaux, 33
Biel, Gabriel, 106
birds, 21, 138, 166, 169, 177, 182
bishops, 40, 42, 107, 121, 134, 143, 164
Black Cloister, 2, 136n19
Bohemians, 32, 47, 72
books, 3, 42, 54–57, 64, 106, 119, 123, 126–27, 136, 143, 147, 149, 167
Bora, Katherine von. *See* Luther, Katherine
Bucer, Martin, 46, 143

Cajetan, Cardinal, 144n30
catechism, 39, 57, 129, 143
celibacy, 170, 177
ceremonies, 23, 41, 73, 101, 185
certainty, 19, 57, 101
children, 2, 21, 24, 39, 45, 51, 53, 73–74, 76–77, 79, 81, 84, 103, 121, 123, 135, 139–40, 151, 152–53, 156, 157–58, 163–65, 173, 176, 178–79, 181–82, 186
Christ, 1, 5–7, 8–11, 13–19,

189

22–25, 29, 30–38, 44–48,
52–55, 58–59, 62, 65–69,
72–83, 85n27, 86, 90–91,
93–94, 96–101, 103, 105–6,
111–16, 118–19, 121, 123,
128–29, 132, 134–36, 138–39,
141, 147–49, 153–54, 158–62,
164, 167, 174–75, 178–83
Christmas, 180, 181
Compostella, 21
confession, 5, 25, 47, 72, 78, 83, 86, 139, 171
conscience, 8, 10, 16, 19, 26, 48, 64, 82, 100, 101–2, 121–22, 129, 145, 148
consecration, 103–4
council, 41, 105n17, 107, 121, 131, 140
creation, 22, 55, 56, 86–87, 112, 118, 126, 156, 165, 173, 179, 180–82, 184
cross, sign of the, 140

day, last, 32, 95, 100, 104, 128, 134, 160, 186
demons, 92, 120, 164, 165–66
devil, 9, 13, 14–17, 24–25, 27, 32, 53, 56, 58, 62, 74, 90–92, 99, 112, 114, 118, 120, 122, 128, 131–33, 135, 137, 138–42, 149, 153, 155, 158–63, 165, 174–76, 182, 185, 187
Dietrich, Veit, 155n1
Dionysius the Areopagite, 98
discipline, 149, 156

doctrine, 9, 23, 41, 44, 46, 100, 104, 113–14, 119, 123, 138, 167
doubt, 7, 8–9, 19, 33, 57, 76, 94, 101, 104, 127, 138–39, 185
dreams, 43, 132–33

Eck, John, 91, 104, 121
Erasmus, Desiderius, 11, 32, 33, 42, 126
excommunication, 44, 138
experience, 3, 7, 11, 16, 32, 68, 89, 97–98, 100, 113, 127, 129, 134, 136, 140–41, 146–47, 156, 166, 170, 175

faith, 1, 5, 7, 9, 11–12, 14, 18–22, 25, 26–28, 32, 45, 51–52, 56–58, 64, 66–67, 69, 72, 75, 78–80, 85–86, 90, 94, 99–101, 104–5, 108–9, 111–14, 122–23, 126, 129, 139, 146–47, 160–61, 176–77, 179, 181–82, 184
fall, the, 8–9, 13, 61, 64, 94, 115, 172, 181
fasting, 23, 148
fellowship, 22, 82, 128, 137n21, 161, 167, 174, 179
firearms, 172
fish, 156, 169
forgiveness, 1, 5, 9, 12, 15, 17, 54, 83, 93, 94, 95, 110–11, 128, 157, 160, 174–75, 179

games, 171

INDEX

George of Saxony, Duke, 8, 100, 107, 164
God: knowledge of, 18, 20, 48, 91–92, 97; omnipresence, 91; service of, 13; way to speak, 34–35; wrath of, 43, 61, 109, 114, 129, 146, 168, 182
gospel, 3, 11, 15–16, 21, 37, 41–43, 48, 53–55, 67–69, 89, 94, 97, 99, 101–2, 109, 111–12, 127, 138, 146, 157, 159, 162, 167, 174–75, 186
government: civil, 54, 101

heaven, 13, 20, 26, 33, 35, 43, 51–54, 56, 61, 65, 74, 77, 86, 94, 111, 113, 117, 119–20, 128–29, 131, 142, 150, 152, 160, 161, 171, 176, 180, 183
history, 9, 119, 143, 185
hospitals, 178
Hungarians, 82
Huss, John, 131–32

immortality, 116, 120n37
indulgences, 1, 107, 110, 131, 136, 144n30
Italians, 42, 108, 144, 165, 178

Jerusalem, 21, 63, 67, 112
Jews, 9, 10, 18, 31, 55, 60, 64, 66–67, 69, 73, 75–76, 82, 95–96, 113–14, 162
John Frederick of Saxony, elector, 2, 136n19, 138n25

judgment, last, 67, 74, 100, 115, 159, 186. *See also* day, last
justification, 19, 23, 59, 89–90, 102–3, 110–11, 120, 128, 148

kingdoms, two, 101

laity, 45, 80
law, 10, 13, 15–16, 19, 27, 43–44, 48–49, 53–54, 60, 62–63, 67–68, 74, 78–79, 84, 89–90, 94–98, 101–2, 109, 111–12, 122, 132, 146, 157, 173–75
lawyer, 43n21, 93, 98–99, 186
left-wing, 72
life, future, 23–24, 156–57, 166–67, 179, 180
Lord's Supper, 5n1, 35, 72, 76, 78, 80, 85n28, 100
love, 6, 11–12, 13, 25, 30, 35, 52–53, 68, 93–94, 100, 102, 109, 122–23, 131, 150, 152, 161, 164, 172, 174, 181, 187
Luther, Katherine, von Bora (aka Katy), 2, 3, 24, 35, 49, 118n32, 119n36, 125–26, 133, 135, 138, 155, 159, 168–69, 184
Luther, Magdalene, 150–52
Luther, Martin: on childhood, 117, 168; collected works, 3–4, 143, 147; entrance into the monastery, 127, 140; excommunication, 138; false report of death, 141–42; first mass of, 133, 135, 140; illnesses, 134, 139, 141–42, 146, 179; lectures

191

of, 102n14, 130, 136, 145; as monk, 19–20, 55, 64, 95, 127, 132–34; parents of, 23, 136 162; self-analysis of, 130; "tower experience" of, 100, 146

magistrate, 31, 101, 156
marriage, 2–3, 18–19, 33, 37, 62, 110, 121, 126, 155–57, 162, 165, 168, 170–72, 177, 185–87
Mary, 33, 34, 60–61, 67, 80, 86, 111, 122
mass, 19–20, 23, 81–83, 106, 108, 126, 130, 133–35, 141n29, 147–49
medicine, 92, 141, 142
melancholy, 4, 12, 14, 22, 127–28, 175
Melanchthon, Philip, 17, 21–22, 25n24, 27n26, 37, 41, 46, 58, 65, 90, 102, 105, 113, 118–19, 121, 134–35, 137, 152–53, 163, 170, 177
minister, 19, 30, 35–36, 39–40, 42–43, 47, 49–50, 53, 63, 79, 86, 108, 140, 156, 178
ministry, 3, 29, 31, 33, 38, 126, 131
miracles, 25, 36–37, 92, 113–14, 185
monastery, 3, 67, 121, 127, 133, 140, 148
monks, 2, 20, 22, 41–42, 96, 127, 132n16, 134, 140, 143, 148, 176, 179

music, 159, 160n4, 169–70, 171, 173–74

nature, human, 120, 171

ordination, 40, 79–80, 112

parents, 3, 75, 81, 123, 152, 182, 186
peasants, 52, 92–93, 102n15, 158
physicians, 92, 113, 141, 142, 146, 149, 166, 178
pilgrimage, 21, 148
Plato, 44, 91, 98, 116–17
prayer, 7, 16, 20, 24, 27–28, 51, 57, 69, 76, 93, 103–6, 110, 113, 129, 131–33, 155, 187
preacher, 30, 32–34, 36–40, 42–44, 46–47, 49, 59, 65, 90, 93, 126, 175
preaching, 19, 23, 33, 36–43, 45–46, 49, 57
predestination, 76, 95–96, 104, 114
printer, 147
purgatory, 1, 19, 104–5, 147n36

reason, 8, 13, 20, 64, 86, 89–92, 112–15, 129, 158, 180, 182
reformation, 1–2, 5n2, 16n14, 29n3, 119n35, 127n8, 153n39, 160n4
revenge, 45, 60
riches, 26, 97, 145
righteousness, 1, 18–19, 23–25,

27, 67, 82, 94n6, 95–96, 100, 111, 114, 131, 146

sacramentarians, 35, 57–58, 72, 123
sacraments, 3, 5, 13, 19, 22, 31, 35–36, 40, 48–49, 71, 72–73, 76–80, 82–86, 109n25, 141n29, 171. *See also* baptism; Lord's Supper
sacrifice, 13, 20, 38, 74, 81–82, 135, 141n29
saints, 10, 19, 21, 23, 51, 80, 94, 105, 110, 122, 129, 148, 160, 165
satan. *See* devil
scholastics, 10n6, 51, 106, 115, 143, 184
schools, 66, 92, 153, 187
scriptures, 11, 14, 18n18, 22, 33, 38, 43–44, 49, 51–55, 58, 60–61, 65–66, 68, 87, 89, 92, 93–94, 97, 99–100, 104–7, 112–13, 115–16, 118–21, 128, 132–33, 145, 147, 154, 160–61
sex, 104, 110, 155, 164
sin: original, 71, 110, 171, 183
Smalcald, 24n21, 43, 45, 137n22, 142
solitude, 17–18, 21–22, 175–76
sophistry, 44
sophists, 10, 44, 109, 111–12
soul, 1, 14, 24, 30, 57, 67, 72, 97, 103, 115–17, 119–20, 131, 138, 152, 176, 185
speculation, 55, 92, 104, 180

Staupitz, John, 5, 17, 97, 130
student, 2, 5n2, 7, 23, 41n20, 50, 58, 82, 89, 98, 104–6, 153, 167, 170

theologian/theology, 1, 22n20, 29, 36, 54, 65, 71n1, 89–93, 96–99, 102, 109n24, 115, 118–20, 181
translation, 42, 55, 56
trinity, 86, 112–14, 120
Turks, 54, 74, 94, 96, 112–13, 165

ubiquity, 77
usurers, 48–49
usury, 60, 98

Waldensians, 18–19, 79
widow, 172–73
will, free, 104–5
will, last, 167
wine, 58, 71, 79, 82n20, 84, 85nn27,28, 113, 137, 141n29, 148, 165
women, 37, 46, 49, 61, 76, 84, 125, 164–66
Word of God, 8–9, 15, 22–23, 26, 29–31, 34, 40, 42, 49, 51–54, 56–57, 63–65, 69, 73, 87, 92, 103–5
Worms, Diet of, 3, 131n13, 177n11
worship, 13, 73, 75, 101, 115, 133, 181. *See also* ceremonies

Zwingli, Huldreich, 32, 90, 92

193

www.ingramcontent.com/pod-product-compliance
Ingram Content Group UK Ltd.
Pitfield, Milton Keynes, MK11 3LW, UK
UKHW021327180426
11947UKWH00017B/1476